ADVANCE PRAISE FOR
GEORGE VARNELL: THE LIFE AND TIMES
OF A PIONEERING SPORTSMAN

"George Varnell stood with the tallest of American football giants. The story of his playing for Amos Alonzo Stagg at Chicago, then becoming a sportswriter and leading football official—handling a record eight Rose Bowls—is nicely captured by Jeff Burlingame. This deeply researched book relays the facts about Varnell while imparting the essence of the man, particularly his love of sports and sportsmen."
—*Timothy P. Brown, author of* How Football Became Football

"From football star, Olympic athlete, and multisport coach, George Varnell became one of the nation's foremost authorities on college football as he devoted almost half a century to dual careers as a sports editor and record-setting West Coast football referee. This thoroughly researched, comprehensive, very readable account has it all—and details of his personal life, as well."
—*Jim Price, Pacific Northwest sports historian*

"George Varnell lived the kind of century-filling life that almost sounds like it's made up: star athlete, Olympian, coach, sports writer, editor, and Seattle journalism legend. Jeff Burlingame does an excellent job of putting that life into the historical context of the times. With detailed research and skilled writing, Burlingame has

crafted a compelling book I couldn't put down."
—*Charles R. Cross,* New York Times *bestselling author of* Heavier Than Heaven

"Rowing is the quintessential team sport, and for decades at the University of Washington, that team included George Varnell. Jeff Burlingame has wonderfully captured the energy and spirit of a man who defined our community and did as much for the sport through his writing as anyone."
—*Eric Cohen, University of Washington Rowing historian*

"Much of what I was able to learn about the 1936 University of Washington crew team came to me through the detailed and vibrant reportage of two outstanding sportswriters—Royal Brougham and George Varnell. What many readers of *The Boys in the Boat* may not realize is that both men lived extraordinarily interesting lives. In this well-researched and compelling biography, Jeff Burlingame does a marvelous job of unveiling the rich and intriguing tapestry of George Varnell's life."
—*Daniel James Brown, #1* New York Times *bestselling author of* The Boys in the Boat

GEORGE VARNELL

THE LIFE AND TIMES
OF A PIONEERING SPORTSMAN

JEFF BURLINGAME

Editor: John C. Hughes

Book design: Kirsten Erwin

Cover photo: *Chicago Daily News* Collection,
Chicago History Museum: SDN-002655

Back cover photo: *The Seattle Times*

ISBN: 978-0-578-95024-2

Library of Congress Control Number: 2021924689

First Edition

Tacoma, Washington

For Lisa, Tierney, and Grayson
—my most valuable players.

TABLE OF CONTENTS

George Varnell and his only child, Virginia Elizabeth, inside the now-nonexistent Paradise Ice Caves at Mount Rainier National Park. (Varnell family photo)

FOREWORD

TO MY BROTHER, SISTER, AND ME, George Varnell was "Baba," the only grandfather we ever knew. He used Williams Lectric Shave; liked Burns and Allen, Jack Benny, and *Dragnet* on TV; shook when he laughed; and hid your ice cream bowl when you weren't looking. To our great good fortune, he was very much a part of our lives. Our mother was his only child, and Baba and Nanny (our grandmother) visited us most every Sunday. Upon arrival, Baba changed into work clothes, which were kept in the front hall closet, and proceeded to work in the yard for hours with our dad. It was the only time we saw him without a jacket and tie, his real work clothes. For Sunday lunch, we all would gather in the kitchen. These informal meals usually included vanilla ice cream, a Baba favorite, sometimes accompanied by freshly baked angel food cake. It was here that a grandchild could discover his or her ice cream missing, if only momentarily.

Baba and Nanny's apartment, just off the main commercial street of Seattle's Capitol Hill, was an important place in our youth. There, we never tired of slipping into our grandparents' bedroom, exiting the fire-escape door to descend the winding staircase into the garage, from where we would come back in the main entry, go up a flight of stairs, and ring the front doorbell to be greeted with mock surprise. Overnights were a treat, at least for us, as we displaced Baba and Nanny from their bedroom to the hide-a-bed in the living room. We fell asleep watching the shadows of the trolley buses and streetlights running across the bedroom ceiling. We called those magical shadows "busy lizzies." At Thanksgiving dinner, we'd be delighted to discover a Baba-placed dollar bill when we unfolded our napkins. Today, we still say Baba's grace before holiday meals.

Our grandfather was on the shorter side, about the same height as our grandmother, with a handsome bald head and sun-darkened complexion, and an ample "Varnell nose." He was warm and doting to his grandchildren, but not someone to trifle with, and we always maintained our respect. We would occasionally see a flash of temper, such as when he was behind the wheel. Generally, around his grandchildren, Baba was understated and happy to let others talk, though we still smile about some memorable exceptions, when he referred to a local figure as "so crooked he could sleep in a figure eight," or that another "knew as much about (fill in the blank) as a pig knew about Christmas."

Late into his days, Baba retained a remnant of his athletic gifts, demonstrating quick reflexes with his grandchildren when he would hold his hands under ours, palm to palm, and then try to slap the top of our hands before we could pull them away. Baba didn't talk a lot about his athletic or other sports-related accomplishments. Our grandparents' modest one-bedroom apartment displayed few mementos—no framed photos of Baba in his football or referee uniforms. The top drawer of the desk held our grandmother's collection of swizzle sticks from trips up and down the West Coast, where they traveled together to games Baba covered for the newspaper. Games often were followed by dinners with the home-team coaches and their wives, with whom they developed warm relationships over the years.

Part of our knowledge gap of our grandfather's accomplishments was due to being too young and unaware to ask the questions we would today if given that second chance one never gets. Another part is due to the one thing we never learned anything about from Baba—retirement. He worked into his eighties until he became too sick to work any longer. Not a lot of time to sit around talking about the glory days. The thing we knew most was that he was a sportswriter for *The Seattle Daily Times,* then Seattle's afternoon newspaper, primarily covering University of Washington sports teams. We would see his byline in the newspaper and the weekly cartoon of "Yogi" Varnell, with a wizard hat and crystal-ball, revealing his predictions for that weekend's college football games. We also used some tools of the newspaper trade around the house—round yellow pencils with thick, dark lead, and brown, fibrous scratch paper—known to us simply as "Baba pencils" and "Baba paper."

Looking back, we did have windows into Baba's sportswriting world. I can remember sitting just outside the press ropes at Hec Edmundson Pavilion as Baba kept a running tab of Husky basketball game highlights with two-finger typing on the big, round keys of his black typewriter. My sister, Vinny, and I—and some friends—once received a Baba-led tour of *The Seattle Daily Times*, where we learned how the paper was produced, but maybe more so learned that Baba was a favorite of the office secretaries and of the pressmen and typesetters. We learned the literal meaning of "hot off the press" when we were presented with freshly made metal letter blocks that you had to flip from hand to hand until they cooled down. Our older brother, Pat, was the only one of us to experience the most hallowed ground of Baba's work world—the press box at Husky Stadium—as he was the only grandchild to meet the two strictly enforced entrance requirements: one, you had to be at least sixteen years old, and two, you had to be a male. Pat also worked as an intern in the sports department at *The Times*, providing a little boost in coverage for his high school's sports teams. The closest I got to the press box were the Husky football seats Baba provided, Tunnel 28, Row WW, a treasured location. On a few occasions, I rode with Baba to the game, a trip that included a stop to purchase a special cigar for the attendant at the press parking area.

One thing we knew well about Baba was our mother's great affection for him. She was hardly a "chip off the old block"—she, a precocious English major who entered college at age sixteen, while he was an Olympian and collegiate athlete whose excellence on the playing fields was apparently not matched in the classroom. Yet they were kindred spirits. Among Mom's fondest memories were trips the two of them took together, especially a cross-country train trip that included a stopover in Chicago for Baba to visit his legendary college football coach, Amos Alonzo Stagg. Mother also told us about a Hollywood studio tour that they took when she traveled to Los Angeles with her parents for the 1932 Olympic Games. On the tour, some Hollywood celebrities were eager to talk with noted referee George Varnell about a call he had made in an important game. Perhaps some wagers had been involved. Baba proceeded to explain the difference between a safety and a touchback.

While our dad played football in high school and loved University of Washington football, it was our mother, who grew up surrounded by sports, who was the bigger sports fan. She always was happy to have a game on in any season, though despite her father's long career as an impartial referee, Mom always had a rooting interest, which often sent her out of the room into the hallway, so as not to jinx her team by watching. She had modest athletic abilities, but she definitely inherited the Varnell sports gene, which was passed on in abundance to her father's grandchildren and great-grandchildren, who as a group competed in nearly all the sports George Varnell excelled in, and also did sports reporting, both in print and on radio.

It is others who have brought to life the fullness of our grandfather's sports legacy. The late Lynn Borland, in his biography of University of Washington football Coach Gil Dobie, *Pursuit of Perfection*, tells the fascinating story of Coach Dobie, who went undefeated in nine years as UW football coach from 1908-16 before being fired. Thanks to Lynn's meticulous research, George Varnell's name often appears in the book, as he was the referee for many of Coach Dobie's games, including some of the most important ones in the history of West Coast football. We learned from Lynn of our grandfather's friendship with Coach Dobie, and my brother and I were privileged to help in Lynn's successful effort to have Coach Dobie honored with a plaque at Husky Stadium. Lynn's book was one of the inspirations for this book, and we know he would be delighted that a George Varnell biography now has been written.

My grandfather's name also appears in Daniel James Brown's remarkable best-seller, *The Boys in the Boat*, which tells the story of the 1936 University of Washington crew that won the Olympic gold medal in Germany under Hitler's eyes. We knew that rowing held a special place in our grandfather's heart, a fact reinforced each time we would meet a UW rower from the early 1960s or before and see him light up when we asked whether he knew George Varnell. Family members have had the honor on a number of occasions to present the George M. Varnell Trophy, annually awarded to the winner of UW's men's Class Day race. But it was downright thrilling to see our grandfather referenced in multiple places in *The Boys in the Boat*, including the epic passage describing the dramatic 1936 national championship race in Poughkeepsie, New York, where Baba was among those in the observation train following the race, along with UW coaches, alums, and other members of the press corps. My brother and I have had the sublime pleasure of hearing Mr. Brown read that passage aloud.

While our mother had told us Baba had been the football coach at Gonzaga University in Spokane, it was my work colleague at the Seattle Center, and noted Seattle sports historian, Russ Dille who told me that my grandfather was the first basketball coach at Gonzaga, a fact that has been a special point of pride given Gonzaga's amazing basketball accomplishments over the last two-plus decades. Baba would truly be amazed and delighted by that success.

And now Jeff Burlingame has researched and written a biography of our grandfather, chronicling his life in the sports world from elite athlete to coach to referee to sportswriter. Baba as athlete is the part we grandchildren knew the least about, and Jeff has given us a much greater appreciation for who that person was, including some wonderful photos of a young man we did not know, but whose facial resemblance to our mother is heartwarmingly evident. We also are very much intrigued by a mysterious Kentucky chapter in Baba's life, and bemused by some Varnell family history that is definitely more notorious than glorious. In all, this book has given us a fuller and greater appreciation for George Varnell, well beyond

"Baba," whose memory we carry with us with great affection. We are most grateful to Jeff for his outstanding research and writing. We are delighted to have this biography, and we hope you enjoy it as well.

Ned Dunn, grandson of George Varnell
January 2023

1

THE FALL BEFORE THE RISE

TO MOST IN THE PANATHENAIC STADIUM crowd of 80,000, Pierre de Coubertin was just another spectator jostling to glimpse the top athletes and dignitaries from fourteen nations. Only a handful present knew his importance: that without him, this historic moment would not have unfolded. It was April 6, 1896, inside an ancient marble landmark built on a site in Athens, Greece, that first had echoed to cheering in the sixth century B.C. The first Modern Olympics—chiefly Coubertin's doing—were about to begin.

For a decade, the dapper and diminutive thirty-three-year-old French educator had championed, far and wide, the revival of this storied event. The Olympics, he believed, would allow countries to settle differences on athletic fields rather than battlefields, just as they had for centuries in antiquity until the rise of Christianity led to the prohibition of the games, seen as steeped in paganism. That this Olympic revival was taking place on Easter Monday—the day

Pierre de Coubertin, "Father of the Modern Olympics," refused to attend the 1904 St. Louis Olympics, in which George Varnell competed. (James E. Sullivan: Spalding's Official Athletic Almanac for 1905)

after the biblical resurrection—seemed both ironic and fitting. After 1,500 years, lithe young men from many countries once again paraded into an arena, hoping to win laurels for their speed and strength. These Olympics were Coubertin's, and he theirs, for all ten competition-filled days.

Four years later, at the turn of the century, Coubertin was ubiquitous in Paris, which that year hosted both the Olympics and the World's Fair. There, he famously rode his motorized tricycle from one end of his birth city to another. To and fro he went through the crowds, from Bois de Boulogne to Bois de Vincennes, to watch the croquet players, cyclists, runners, and gymnasts from twenty-eight countries compete for medals. His baby had doubled in size.

Yet in 1904, when the third installment of the Modern Olympics opened in St. Louis, Missouri, Coubertin was nowhere to be found. Just forty-one years old and as strong an Olympics promoter as ever, he was missing from the opening ceremony in May, and did not attend any of the ninety-five events held throughout the next five months. The proud "Father of the Modern Olympics," as Coubertin had come to be known, had ended his involvement with the St. Louis Games a year earlier. The host city was the reason.

"I harboured great resentment against the town for the disillusionment caused by my first sight of the junction of the Missouri and the Mississippi rivers," Coubertin wrote in his memoirs. St. Louis, he wrote, failed to live up to author James Fenimore Cooper's colorful accounts "… of the setting where these rivers with their strange resounding names actually met!" There was "no beauty, no originality," Coubertin wrote. "I had a sort of presentiment that the Olympiad would match the mediocrity of the town."[1]

Coubertin's contempt for the St. Louis Games was not simply due to the incongruence between one author's fulsome depictions of the American West and what his own eyes saw during a brief visit to the city. He also long had preferred that America's first Olympics be held in Chicago or New York City.

In 1901, Coubertin thus had celebrated when the International Olympic Committee—IOC for short—had unanimously awarded the 1904 games to Chicago over St. Louis, the only other United States city to submit a bid. The committee, including Coubertin, had resolved that Chicago, a metropolis three times larger than St. Louis, would be easier for international travelers to access, and the stellar reputation Chicago had earned by hosting the 1893 World's Fair also would help attract visitors.

Chicagoans had celebrated the news, too. At the University of Chicago, thousands of students took to their football field, dancing and singing around a celebratory bonfire. The *Chicago Tribune* gloated: "St. Louis tried to get the Olympian games. But the international committee seems to have decided that St. Louis wouldn't know what to do with them."[2] Almost immediately, plans were drawn and architects contracted to build a 70,000-seat, retractable-roof stadium adjacent to Lake Michigan. Hyde Park, on the city's South Side, was selected as the site of the expansive, soon-to-be-built Olympic village.

St. Louis conceded defeat, but an interesting turn of events soon inspired its city leaders to reignite the battle for the 1904 Olympics. It all began when St. Louis's own World's Fair was switched from 1903—the 100th anniversary of the Louisiana Purchase—to 1904 to accommodate additional construction of the fair's massive grounds and also to allow more countries the chance to participate. "We could have held as great a fair in 1903 as was ever held anywhere in the world. But we can hold a greater fair than any in history if we postpone it one more year,"[3] the fair's president, former Missouri Governor David R. Francis, said in 1902 shortly after a White House meeting on the subject with President Theodore Roosevelt. The biggest driver of the postponement, according to brewing magnate and fair board member Adolphus Busch, was that Japan's own national fair in 1903 would stop its athletes and citizens from coming to St. Louis.

St. Louis's date change meant it and Chicago would be in direct competition for national and international visitors in 1904. Back then, the Olympics were a paltry draw compared to a World's Fair—particularly a World's Fair in which organizers had planned to stage their own athletic events backed by the influential Amateur Athletic Union. And if the Olympics were relegated to playing second fiddle to a World's Fair for the second straight time, it could prove disastrous to the fledgling games. The IOC realized this and reluctantly agreed to transfer the 1904 Games from Chicago to St. Louis.

Once again, thousands of University of Chicago students gathered on their football field and lit a bonfire. This time, the gathering nearly ended in a riot.[4]

THE STILL-BITTER PIERRE DE COUBERTIN remained half a world away on August 31, 1904, as a young American named George Varnell prepped for the race of his life. Wearing white shorts and a white athletic tank top embroidered with a large "C" inside a circle—the emblem of the Chicago Athletic Association—Varnell stepped to the starting line of the third lane of the one-third-mile dirt track at St. Louis's Washington University.

Though Varnell likely did not know it, Coubertin's absence was the chief reason he was there. Shifting the games to St. Louis had caused the event to lose much of its appeal; only twelve countries sent athletes to compete, and only sixty of the 650 competitors were from outside North America. Had international participation been as strong as it had been four years earlier in Paris, Varnell

Spectators rest in the stands at Washington University in St. Louis
during the 1904 Olympics. (Missouri Historical Society)

would not have made the cut. He was an excellent all-around athlete, but certainly not an elite international hurdler.

Yet there he was, a twenty-two-year-old Chicago native, multisport star, and recent University of Chicago enrollee, stretching
his legs to flirt with fame in the finals of the 400-meter hurdles.
Varnell had been named to the team only a few weeks earlier, and
then trained rigorously on Chicago's Marshall Field* with more
than a dozen others from his school and the universities of Michigan, Purdue, Illinois, and Indiana. He and his teammates—including French marathoner Albert Corey—all were in St. Louis
competing for the Chicago Athletic Association.

Varnell's midmorning race was a four-person, all-American
affair held in front of 10,000 spectators standing trackside and seat-

---

*The University of Chicago's Marshall Field was named after local merchant Marshall Field (1834-
1906), who donated the land to the university.

ed in concrete stands. To Varnell's right, in lane four, stood Harry Hillman of the New York Athletic Club. Two days earlier, Hillman had set an Olympic record of 49.2 seconds to win gold in the 400 meters.

To Varnell's far left, in lane one, was the Milwaukee Athletic Club's George Poage, a former conference champion at the University of Wisconsin. Poage had matched Hillman stride for stride for 300 meters of that 400 meters, before fading and finishing sixth. Still, Poage had earned a place in Olympic history earlier in the Games when, simply by running in a heat of the 60-meter sprint, he became the first Black competitor in Olympics history. To Varnell's immediate left, in lane two, was his Chicago Athletic Association teammate, Frank Waller, who had finished second to Hillman in the 400.

At the crack of the starter's pistol, the boyish-looking Hillman took the lead, safely remaining there, even after knocking over the third hurdle, until he tripped on and nearly tumbled over the final barrier. The stumble allowed Waller to draw even, yet Hillman pulled away to win in a world-record time of 53 seconds. Waller finished a half step behind. Poage finished a distant third, achieving another milestone: the first Black man to win an Olympic medal.

All historical accounts list Varnell as the fourth-place finisher of four. None provides his time, but several describe the race in detail, calling it even between the four men most of the way. One narrative, written years later by historian Bill Mallon, notes that Varnell tripped and fell at the seventh hurdle and suggested he might not have finished at all.[5] Only two photos of the race are known to exist, both snapped from just beyond the finish. The clearest of the two black-and-white shots shows a bespectacled Hillman easing up after crossing the white-chalk finish line, as Waller futilely extends his chest to edge him out. Poage is in the middle of a casual stride about halfway between the final hurdle and the finish. Varnell is nowhere to be seen.

Hillman, Waller, and Poage again are the focus of the second photo, although this time Varnell can be spotted far in the distance, his left arm raised as he leaps over the ninth of the ten wooden hurdles, proving that he did rise from his fall. Newspaper accounts reported that the Chicago Athletic Association received one point in the team standings from Varnell, confirming he did indeed cross the finish line.

Scratched, bruised, and somewhat shocked by the rare overwhelming defeat, Varnell dusted himself off and stepped to the side of the track. There was no time for sulking. He had another race the next day, but first he had to walk across the field to cheer for others. That was George Varnell's way.

SON OF A PRINCE

BILLY CLUBS, CROWBARS, AND SLEDGEHAMMERS in their hands and justice on their minds, a dozen of Detective Matt Pinkerton's finest—including three pugnacious men with "large fighting reputation[s]"[1]—crept inside the front door of Varnell's Gaming House and soft-stepped up the wooden stairs to the second floor.

Almost three years old on this Tuesday, September 18, 1894, Harry Varnell's crowded establishment was an unparalleled jewel on the seamy stretch of Chicago's Clark Street dubbed Gambler's Row. It was a nickname given for several reasons. The most obvious: Dozens of gaming houses lined the street. The not-so obvious: Those who ventured there after dusk were gambling in one form or another. Either with their money, or with their lives.

By day, this downtown area just south of the Chicago River near Whiskey Row and the Vice District ebbed and flowed with the

Varnell's Gaming House on Clark Street in Chicago was so extravagant that thousands of people attended its grand opening in October 1891. (Belgravia Publishing, Newberry Library Microfilm)

legitimate business activity of a major city that had in the previous year realized a big boom and also a big bust. In 1893, Chicago's World's Fair had attracted twenty-five million visitors—and thirty-five million of their dollars. Yet that year also saw the onset of a crippling national depression—the Panic of 1893, in which hundreds of banks and railroads that called on Chicago as their major hub had failed.

Come nighttime, business still was robust on Gambler's Row, its gaslit streets providing cover for pimps and panel houses in which prostitutes' rooms were "bare except for a bed and a single chair set against the wall." While a client hung his clothes on that strategically placed chair, a "creeper" peering through a hole in the wall would gauge "the peak of [the client's] preoccupation," then "slide open a hidden panel just above the chair and pick his wallet and watch."[2] Though illicit activities had existed in Chicago long before the World's Fair, the exposition had generated a bumper crop of decadence. Gamblers, for example, arrived from across the world, seeking opportunity among unsuspecting visitors to the wide-open Midwestern metropolis. Paid-off police often looked the other way.

Varnell's Gaming House, open 'round the clock, was the epitome of Gilded Age grandeur: luminous and inoffensive on the surface, yet tinged with internal immorality and supported by a semi-crooked foundation. In an era when a typical Chicago laborer grossed $400 a year, Harry "Prince Hal" Varnell had spent $50,000 on his lighting and furnishings alone. So grand was Prince Hal's establishment that its October 1891 opening had drawn coverage from newspapers across the Midwest. One reported:

> [O]ver 3,000 visiting guests assembled to inaugurate the auspicious opening of the place, and 3,000 more agreeably and delightedly surprised men were never seen in this or any other city. The woodwork and fixtures are of beautifully carved mahogany, while the wainscoting is of pure Mexican onyx. The floor, of Florentine mosaic, is laid in oriental patterns, the walls and ceilings decorated in Lapillo Novo, and the partition screens are made of mahogany, and are finished with an [sic] unique metallic sash, composed of beveled glass and antique silver. This feature of the decorator's art is the finest effect ever produced … The quality of wines, liquors and cigars is unexcelled, and regular artists are employed to dispense the liquid refreshments to a large patronage.[3]

Ostentation was something Varnell certainly could afford. His reported annual income—which included profits from his near-monopoly on liquor distribution and betting at horse-racing tracks in Northern Illinois and Indiana—was around $1 million [roughly $34,000,000 in 2022 dollars].[4] The annual payroll at his gaming house was $171,000.[5]

This drawing from the Chicago Tribune shows some of the thousands of
onlookers gathered outside Varnell's Gaming House during a massive raid
conducted on September 18, 1894. (The Chicago Tribune)

FIRST UP THE STAIRS was the superintendent of Pinkerton's agency, Detective Harvey Devereaux, closely followed by a constable named Reinke, who held in his shirt pocket the search warrant his boss had persuaded a judge to sign minutes earlier. Illegal activities were taking place inside Varnell's, Pinkerton had solemnly sworn.

Those first two agents and the ten others who followed were operating under orders of The Civic Federation, a philanthropy formed by a group of powerful Chicagoans intent on cleaning up their fair city. The raid on Varnell's was the federation's first ordered attack on organized gambling. It showed.

Constable Reinke paused just inside the wide-open, weighty door at the top of the stairs. Through the thick cigar smoke, he saw 250 men seated at the faro, hazard, roulette, and stud poker tables. Pulling the warrant from his pocket, he began reading, half-shouting over the piano music:

"Being duly sworn ..."

A holler from across the room—"C'mon, boys!"—interrupted the recitation. Harry Varnell's men had been tipped off.

Some fifty gamblers and gangsters armed with blackjacks, canes, and revolvers sprung from a side hallway and rushed head-first into Pinkerton's outnumbered men. Someone barred the thick oaken door. Dozens of Pinkerton's backups, waiting out on Clark Street among the onlookers, were useless.

An hour-long melee ensued, during which Pinkerton's reinforcements finally busted through, making their way past the dozens of shell-shocked patrons fleeing down the stairs. The brawl spilled into the alley behind the building, where Varnell and Pinkerton were arguing nose to nose.

By that point, thousands of onlookers had gathered. Many stuck around after the scene cleared to recap what they had witnessed to anyone who cared to listen, including newspaper reporters. Police, although on scene almost immediately, took no part in the fray, other than to suppress the crowds, "just as they do at large fires," read the next day's *Chicago Tribune*. "Bloody war waged in the gambling-room up-stairs, gamblers and Federation agents fought furiously … but not a finger did any policeman raise to end the conflict."[6]

Arrests *were* made—but only of Pinkerton's men. Pinkerton was arrested, too, but broke free while being transported to the police station and ran to the office of the judge who had signed the warrant for the raid. Pinkerton was allowed to call on a bondsman and released the detective as soon as bail money was promised.

Varnell dusted himself off, reentered his establishment, and declared the commotion over. Shortly, reported the *Tribune*, "[A]ll the games were running at Varnell's as usual. The raiders had not secured a chip. The doors were wide open, the automatic piano was in operation, and 250 men and boys scored for good seats at the table."[7]

A year and a half earlier, Chicago police had conducted a raid of their own on Varnell's. They had confiscated card tables and arrested sixty-seven men—all of whom were bailed out by Varnell within two hours. "This doesn't bother us much,"[8] one of Varnell's managers said at the time. In the short-term, he was correct. However, the persistence of The Civic Federation and a police administration hellbent on abolishing public gaming soon did "bother" Varnell and his workers, as well as the dozens of other organized-gambling proprietors along Gambler's Row.

In 1896, a lengthy list of temporarily shuttered gambling operations was published in the *Tribune*, with Varnell's luxurious Clark Street parlor listed three times. Illegal gambling continued to flourish in Chicago for the rest of the nineteenth century and well into the twentieth, but the police and other organizations had helped push it out of downtown to the suburbs.

HARRY ANTWAINE VARNELL'S run-ins with the law were numerous and notorious, yet his reputation and riches always remained untouched. The company he kept had much to do with that. At the time of the Pinkerton-led raid in 1894, Varnell had lived in Chicago all but three of his forty-three years, having arrived from Wisconsin via Iowa with his young parents, New York-born farmer John Henry Varnel and Elizabeth "Eliza" Jane (Fredendall) Varnel, the one-L'ed spelling simply an alternative take on a family name derived from the words "fern" and "hill."

In Wisconsin, the Varnels had become friends with neighbors Daniel and Ann Gilrye Muir, heads of a large family of fellow farmers who had emigrated from Scotland in the 1840s. When the Varnells moved to Chicago, they remained in touch with the Muirs, visiting when they returned to Wisconsin and, at other times, corresponding via letters. Harry and the third-born of the eight Muir children, John, did at least some of the writing. In January 1863, Harry sent one such letter three weeks before his thirteenth birthday, telling twenty-four-year-old John Muir that he had a small French pony and also updating him on Chicago's unseasonably warm weather, a "sickening"[9] climate in which "persons are dying every day"[10] and filling neighboring homes with sadness. Two days later, on the backside of Harry's letter, his mother tacked on a few thoughts:

> If you come to Chicago please call and see us. Mr. Varnel is well and hard to work. I hope he will try to be more steady than in other days. Oh may God help us to do our duty in the fear of sudden destruction! It is sickly here—smallpox and fevers. … Remember me, John, in your secret devotion, that I fall not by the way. Write soon.[11]

When Harry's letter arrived at the Muir home, located on Fountain Lake Farm outside the town of Montello, its recipient was fifty miles south in Madison, studying chemistry and botany at the University of Wisconsin on his way to becoming the most famous naturalist in American history. John Muir, who died in 1914 at age seventy-six, became the person many credit for the existence of Mount Rainier, Sequoia, Grand Canyon, and Yosemite national parks. Today, his family farm is a historic landmark and is listed on the National Register of Historic Places. The letter Harry wrote is one of nearly 7,000 such pieces of correspondence stored in Muir-related collections housed at dozens of academic institutions in the United States.

Harry's letter to John Muir said he was earning two dollars a week working at Palmer's dry goods store. A short time later, Harry, an only child and an excellent student, began supporting his mother after the death of his father, who had left farming for a career as a butcher, then as a financial bondsman. At sixteen, Harry started his own meat-packing business, then he attended a business college, partnered in a cornice-manufacturing business, and spent two years as a locksmith. A lifelong Democrat, he long had been active in city and county politics, an involvement that led to his 1884 appointment as warden of the Cook County Insane Asylum in rural Dunning, Illinois.

Harry Varnell had taken advantage of his role as warden. While the asylum's 685 patients spent their days attending classes, cleaning laundry, and growing and harvesting their own food on the 160-acre prairie site, he spent much of his time relaxing and entertaining the county commissioners who had appointed him. Many of those commissioners were asylum regulars, visiting to feast on fine foods and partaking of dances and parties in the warden's extravagant quarters in the three-story brick building. Some commissioners lived there during party-filled weekends. A makeshift clubhouse set up in the drugstore was the group's favorite hangout, and there they lounged on luxurious furniture, dined large, and drank top-shelf liquors—all on the taxpayers.

Unsurprisingly, the asylum's by-the-books physician, Shobal Vail Clevenger Jr., did not think highly of his warden. The son of a famous sculptor and scientist who had dedicated much of his career to the study of the brain and nervous system, Clevenger often wrote to others about his grievances with Harry Varnell. In one such letter, later published in a medical review book, Clevenger told of an occasion when he had suggested to Varnell that patients with mild disorders be separately housed from those prone to violence. Varnell responded, "To hell with the damned cranks. They are cattle to me, and I don't give a damn for them and am here for boodle. I'm going to make a pile out of the bughouse, and start a big sporting place in the city."[12] The medical book's author further described the asylum's wild weekend parties: "As soon as it grew dark, gangsters and their women arrive, keeping up night-long orgies that made the inmates furious for want of sleep. Sometimes they would amuse patients by shouting, 'Fire!' It must have been a curious sight for Clevenger to watch these thugs and sluts dancing on the patients' health and on the people's money."[13] One of Dr. Clevenger's assistants, the author wrote, was fired by Varnell a month into his job after the assistant discovered "maggots in a festering ulcer" in one patient and reported it to Warden Varnell, who "threatened to shoot him if he ever saw him again."[14] Also according to the book, Varnell shuttled inmates to the polls each election season, forcing them to vote for his chosen candidates: "[In November 1884] in the second precinct of Norwood Park there registered a total of 129 voters, but under Varnell's adroit management 225 votes were cast, 207 for his ticket."[15]

In February 1887, the *Chicago Tribune* called out Varnell and the county commissioners for the profligacy at the asylum and its adjacent mental hospital:

> These are the ones who live on oysters, bananas, and strawberries, and drink the wine and liquors. … [The employees] and their families occupy the best rooms in these great buildings, and it is they who are fed on the expensive dainties … it is also easy to see for whom the damask lambrequins, the lace curtains, the Brussels carpets, the Persian rugs, have been purchased. The poor, the lunatics, and the sick have fared none too well, but those who have been hired to take care of them have lived in luxury.[16]

Varnell officially earned $166.66 a month for running the asylum, but his unofficial take, padded by bribes and kickbacks, likely was a great deal larger.

The *Tribune* continued investigating the alleged misappropriation of public funds, and published a large, tabloidesque front-page story headlined "Extravagant Varnell." The article insinuated that Varnell—married and living at the asylum with his four children— was buying gifts for, and having an affair with, a "pretty little woman of maybe 25—maybe more" named Mrs. Belcher, who had Varnell's photo on her home's mantel and was "small and ladylike, with tender blue eyes, and a babyish face surmounted by a mass of tiny clustering curls."[17] Varnell responded by filing a libel suit against the paper and cursing out a reporter he ran into at a public meeting. The newspaper then dug in: "[T]here is one frequenter of the County Board rooms who can use more and worse profanity in five minutes than [others] could in half an hour. That genius is Harry Varnell. … He could lick the reporter, he said, with his two hands tied behind his back."[18]

The following month, Varnell and several others were indicted

The registry from the Joliet Correctional Center includes inmate No. 8833, Harry Varnell, who spent two years in the Cook County, Illinois, facility in a shared four-by-seven-foot cell. Previously, the facility had been home to Civil War prisoners and, later, it held several notorious criminals, including serial killer John Wayne Gacy. (Joliet Prison Registry, Illinois State Library Archives)

for conspiring to defraud Cook County. The weeks-long trial became known as The Great Boodle Trial, and was one of the largest corruption scandals of the nineteenth century. All the defendants, except two who had agreed to assist the prosecution, were convicted. Seven of them—Varnell included—were sentenced to two years in a state prison southwest of Chicago at Joliet. According to prison records, the hazel-eyed, brown-haired Varnell checked in at five-feet, eight-inches tall and 220 pounds.

The August 1887 verdict did little to suppress the *Chicago Tribune's* focus on Varnell. In December, while Varnell was behind bars, the paper published "Harry Varnell's 'Boodle,'" an article examining his financials. "Many of the other boodlers may have squandered all of their hard stealings, but he hid his share away for a rainy day," the paper wrote. "He has money and lots of it."[19] The story also described a scene that had occurred in a local bank a day before the verdict. "Handsomely attired in a long silk-plus cloak," a lady identified as Mrs. Varnell withdrew all the contents from Varnell's safe deposit box. "[S]he reached in her hand and drew out a large envelope. … to the great astonishment of the reporter the envelope contained nice, clean, crisp bank bills. They were not ones and twos, but of a much greater denomination."[20]

Varnell wasted little time once they released him and the other convicted boodlers from prison. A *Tribune* reporter witnessed that release, detailing it for a February 11 front-page story: "Varnell was the best-looking man of the lot, of course. Prison life has not left a mark upon the handsome face of the asylum warden. He wore a broad slouch hat, a dark frock coat, brown trousers, and a seal-skin-trimmed overcoat. A magnificent diamond gleamed in his shirt front."[21] Varnell took a car out of the suburbs and hopped a train to Chicago, where he was met on arrival by "… his pale wife (who) ran forward with outstretched arms, and the returned exile gathered her in with a gruff attempt to say something and kissed her. Friends hurried the couple to a carriage and they were driven to their home on West Harrison Street."[22] Varnell began designing his elaborate Clark Street gaming room, which opened the following year.

LITTLE AFFECTION IS EVIDENT in the first Varnell family portrait taken following its patriarch's release from prison. At top left staring into the distance stands heavy-set Harry in a tailored vest and jacket, his dark, thick mustache disconnected from his bushier goatee. To Harry's immediate left is his identically dressed seventeen-year-old son, Claude, who is turned toward his father but gazing past him into the center of the high-ceilinged room. Harry's first-born, Claude, already was involved in organized gambling. In fact, shortly after the 1894 Pinkerton raid on his father's place, Claude was arrested in a raid on a separate Clark Street poolroom. Claude gave police a fake name, though most knew he was the son of the notorious Prince Hal, who bailed him out a short time later.[23]

To Claude's left is the grinning face of thirteen-year-old Harry Jr., who is standing behind his seated ten-year-old sister, Edna. In the frame's center, resting in a high-backed wooden chair, is the "handsomely attired" matriarch, who a little more than two years prior had cleaned out her husband's safe deposit box while he was in prison. The Ohio-born Episcopalian, Eliza "Lillie" Favor, had married Harry Varnell twenty years earlier, when she was nineteen. The regal chair in which she was seated was befitting of the short, curly-haired woman who could boast of a distinguished lin-

The Varnell family in the early 1890s included, top row from left, Harry, Claude, and Harry Jr.; and, seated, George, Eliza, and Edna. (Varnell family photo)

eage. Lillie was the daughter of a Civil War veteran, granddaughter of a New Hampshire physician, and descendant of several generations of upper-class French Huguenots who once fled religious persecution in their homeland and ended up in Massachusetts. Like her ancestors, Lillie had faced adversity with fortitude. During her husband's numerous absences, she had singlehandedly raised several children and had endured the loss of her second-born, daughter Maud, who had died at age three.

The youngest Varnell, seven-year-old George Marshall—the future Olympic athlete—is seated at the footstool of his mother's chair, his left hand holding open the pages of a Bible. George, born August 10, 1882, did not know his father well, having been just two years old when his family moved into the insane asylum and barely five when his father was sentenced to prison. Yet George still possessed the same fun-loving spirit and passion for lake fishing his oft-absent father had.

As fathers go, Harry Varnell was physically and emotionally distant, but his wealth afforded his children better opportunities than most. Claude and Harry Jr. were raised with expensive bicycles, which they learned to race until they became youth champions. Claude also was a star baseball player and, as one might expect from a child who grew up in gaming halls, a billiards wizard, too. George took tennis and swimming lessons, played baseball and football, and became a star runner.

As the Varnell children grew, so too did the success of The Civic Federation's campaign to restrict Chicago's gambling establishments. By the mid-1890s, many such spots on Gambler's Row had been shuttered. In December 1894, three months after the bloody standoff with Harry Varnell's men, the federation finally conquered Varnell's Gaming House, and Mayor John P. Hopkins ordered the doors locked. The establishment's expensive contents—the onyx wainscoting, the mosaic flooring, the velvet-topped card tables— were consigned to mildew and darkness until the doors were unchained a couple years later and the items either sold at auction or given away.[24]

The loss of his gaming room placed Harry Varnell at home in the family's midsize rental apartment above a roadhouse at 4101 North Clark Street for longer periods. Reduced to idleness, he grew depressed and ate too much. On September 12, 1898—nearly four years to the day of the infamous Pinkerton raid on his gaming room—he died in the apartment at age forty-seven from "neuralgia of the heart." His obituary in the *Chicago Tribune* reported that his death was expected, as he had "increased so much in weight during the last four or five years that his friends predicted that either heart disease or apoplexy would carry him off."[25] Despite the newspaper's longstanding clash with Varnell, the obituary characterized the deceased as a kind and sympathetic individual. His demeanor "endeared him to many and made him blind to his faults."[25] Another eulogy reported:

> Among all the sorts of (odd people) who have floated and wriggled to the surface of Cook County politics in the way of professional spoils-seeking ward bosses the most admirable type was this amiable, humorous saloonkeeper and gambler. ... In a way, Varnell was a victim. Given his jovial disposition and the well-known limitations of his moral and mental faculties, he might almost be said to have been an innocent sufferer from the astounding system.[27]

Harry Varnell's memorial service was held at home, his wife and all five of their children—including five-year-old, Goldilocks-haired Marjorie—on hand. Six months later, a picture of him appeared on the lead page of the third section of the Sunday *Chicago Inter Ocean* alongside photos of six other dead men. All seven had at one time been intimately linked to Chicago's Garfield Park horse-racing track. The paper hypothesized that their deaths might have been related to some sort of conspiracy. As for Varnell, the paper wrote that those looking for him after each day's racing had ended could almost always find him in a room in the grandstands:

The Varnell family always dressed to the nines, as evidenced by these two photographs of a young George. Dressing sharply was a character trait George would carry with him his entire life. (Varnell family photos)

The searcher coming to the door of the room often saw a spectacle he could never forget. On each side of the table were placed the rotund—nay, even fat—forms of Colonel [M. Lewis] Clark and Harry Varnell. Before them would be an empty wine bottle, and another perhaps partly filled, while in the middle of the table would be the remains of a tremendous three-inch-thick porterhouse. In the chairs the feasters would sit, their chins dropped on their chests, sleeping audibly, and only to be awakened by sundry punchings and shakings.[28]

After her husband's death, Lillie moved her nearly seventy-year-old widowed mother, Mary Favor, into the apartment, which was by then minus Claude, who had been married four years and had a young daughter of his own named Beryl.

Twenty-one-year-old Harry Jr., an eighth-grade dropout, had become the breadwinner, and was running a saloon adjacent to the former Varnell's Gaming House. Edna, then eighteen, had just finished her formal schooling, as five-year-old Marjorie had just begun hers. Sixteen-year-old George was a high-schooler with a growing reputation as one of Chicago's premier prep athletes.

Each Sunday, Lillie Varnell and most of her children attended the newly built Episcopal Church of the Epiphany on Ashland Avenue (which still stands today as the Epiphany Center for the Arts). Inside the building's sandstone exterior, the family played key roles, including George, who one snowy day in February 1899 served as a cross bearer during a three-hour-long consecration ceremony for the Rev. Theodore Nevin Morrison, the new bishop of the Protestant Episcopal Diocese of Iowa.[29]

That same year, George began his first year at Lewis Institute, a 2,300-student private school on Chicago's West Side. The school that had opened three years earlier was part high school, part junior college, with a curriculum focused on science, literature, and technology. Lewis offered "courses of a kind and character not generally taught in the public schools of the city and with special branches or studies that would be directly useful to students in obtaining a position and occupation for life" and to serve those "who are so circumstanced in life as to be unable without aid and assistance to obtain the instruction and gain access to books and papers of art and science that their future advancement in life requires."[30]

Lewis Institute was the first junior college in the United States, and allowed students to shape their own syllabi, an opportunity public schools of the day did not offer. Tuition was twenty dollars for each twelve-week quarter, and charged only be-

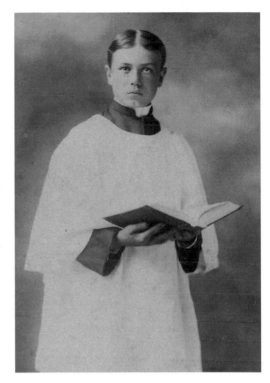

George Varnell was an active member of Chicago's Episcopal Church of the Epiphany. (Varnell family photo)

cause the school felt free tuition would be "... believed to be consistent neither with the design of the Institute nor with that spirit of self-help and self-respect which is the basis of what is best in human character and achievement."[31] An endowment worth some $1.6 million from the estate of Chicagoan Allen Cleveland Lewis funded a majority of Lewis Institute's operations. But the tuition money also was important to the upkeep of the lavish school's facilities, which included a 750-seat lecture hall, a 10,000-book library, and a 10,000-square-foot drawing room with thirteen skylights, each strategically placed so direct sunlight never would shine on any of the room's dozens of drawing tables and blackboards.

George Varnell studied English under recent University of

George Varnell, top left, played center on the
Lewis Institute's basketball team in 1904.
(Lewis Annual, The University of Illinois Library)

Chicago graduate Philemon Bulkley Kohlsaat, and University of Michigan graduates Charlotte Whipple Underwood and Irene Stoddard Baker. Outside the classroom, he grew into a five-sport star, excelling in both singles and doubles tennis, as a doubles-hitting shortstop on the baseball team, as a speedy fullback on the football squad, and as a sprinter and hurdler in track. Despite being only five-feet, eight-inches tall and less than 140 pounds, he also played center on the school's basketball team, which played one early season game against the University of Minnesota. George's ability—and premature balding—often led opposing teams to request identification to prove his eligibility.

After graduating from Lewis Institute's high school in 1902, Varnell entered its School of Arts. He continued competing in several sports and began refereeing high school basketball games. He eventually abandoned basketball and tennis, but stuck with his three best sports: baseball, football, and track. On the gridiron,

Chicago's private Lewis Institute was the first junior college in the United States and, as such, home to a plethora of academic and athletic talent. (Lewis Annual, The University of Illinois Library)

The 1904 Lewis Institute track team featured several of Chicago's best athletes, including future Olympians George Varnell, circled top left, and Bill Hogenson, top right. Hogenson won three Olympic medals shortly after this photo was taken. (Lewis Institute)

Varnell's speedy feet and powerful quads helped him excel in the backfield, alternating between halfback and fullback as his fumble-prone team struggled to score against more talented teams such as Indiana's Culver Military Academy and Northwestern College of Naperville, Illinois.

In track, Varnell conquered all comers in the sprints and the hurdles, the 220-yard low hurdles being his specialty. The 30-inch-high wooden barriers spaced 20 yards apart around the track proved best suited for Varnell's physique: just low enough to easily clear and just far enough apart for his sprinting speed to max out between each one. By the time Varnell was twenty, he was dominating opponents at nearly every regional Amateur Athletic Union event he entered, often winning by 10 or more yards. His personal best in the 220s was 27 seconds, achieved while competing unattached at a summer meet in Chicago in 1903.[32] By comparison, the winner of the USA Track & Field Outdoor Championships that same summer, M.W. Bockman of the Milwaukee Athletic Club, had clocked 26 seconds flat, and the previous year's national champion, Harry Hillman of New York, had finished that championship race in 27.2 seconds.

Varnell's most noteworthy hurdles victory of 1904 came April 30 at an interscholastic meet at Princeton University in New Jersey. There, the recently elected track team captain won the 220-yard hurdles over a field of top preps from thirty other schools and helped lead Lewis Institute to the team title. That year, Lewis Institute was widely believed to have had the best track team in the United States, having won not only the Princeton meet but also finishing on top at equally prestigious meets at Northwestern University and elsewhere.

Lewis Institute's 1904 spring quarter officially ended Friday, June 24, and Varnell graduated with an academic certificate—a couple notches below a modern-day associate's degree—in the field of arts. He had completed courses in English, mathematics, foreign languages, history, and science. By then nearly twenty-two and just entering his athletic prime, Varnell received proposals from several large universities to come compete for them, but in the end determined he was not yet ready to leave behind his widowed mother, his siblings—or his birth city.

3

AMERICA'S GAMES

THERE WAS A TIME WHEN University of Chicago football coach Amos Alonzo Stagg was the most famous and revered sporting figure in the United States, a man whose "mystique surrounded his activities on the gridiron and extended well beyond its perimeter." To many Americans, Stagg personified "a pure, less materialistic, Christian America that had been lost."[1]

Also known as an innovator with a steady moral compass, Stagg, the fifth child of a poor New Jersey laborer, had first achieved renown as a baseball and football All-American at Yale. "Of America's distinguished young men none perhaps are more widely known than A. Alonzo Stagg, the robust Christian athlete of Yale College,"[2] wrote *The Young Men's Journal* in 1890. That was the year Stagg gave up a ministry career to take his first football coaching job at the Young Men's Christian Association Training School in Springfield, Massachusetts.

Pioneering University of Chicago football coach Amos Alonzo Stagg, left, coached college football from the 1890s through to 1946, finishing with a record of 314 wins, 199 losses, and 35 ties. (SDN-051097, Chicago Sun-Times/Chicago Daily News collection, Chicago History Museum)

Stagg left the Young Men's Christian Association two years later, and was appointed head football coach at the newly founded University of Chicago. The hire immediately proved an excellent one. The wavy-haired Stagg roamed the sidelines of the private university's Marshall Field, first as a thirty-year-old player-coach— his body still hardened from the blue-collar work he had done to fund his college education—then strictly as a coach. All the while, he helped revolutionize the still-young sport of football, further differentiating it from its rugby roots by inventing several fundamentals still in use today. Those fundamentals—not all credited solely to Stagg, some scholars say—include the presnap huddle, presnap player motion, the lateral, fake handoffs, onside kicks, padded goalposts, the tackling dummy, the diagramming of plays, and the numbering of uniforms so players could more easily be identified by spectators. Though today other names—Rockne, Bryant, Camp, Heisman—are more quickly named as college gridiron royalty, "A.A." Stagg arguably was more important to the game of football than all of them. Legendary Notre Dame Coach Knute Rockne often made note of that. When asked where his plays came from, Rockne replied, "I took them from Stagg, and Stagg took them from God."[3]

In Stagg's first decade at Chicago, his teams won seventy-seven percent of their games, posting an 111-34-11 record highlighted by a 16-0-2 season in 1899 that included wins over Notre Dame and a Western Conference championship—all while outscoring opponents 505-28. Stagg eventually led the Chicago Maroons to seven conference titles and two national championships.

That extraordinary on-field success was largely due to Stagg's off-field savvy, particularly in the area of player recruitment. In 1902, with the assistance of university president William Rainey Harper, Stagg sold his school on a seven-point recruitment plan. Notably, the plan would create a system to monitor select Illinois and Indiana high school athletes in order to identify blue-chippers and be first in line with an offer.

Chicago's Lewis Institute was one of the university's top feeder schools and, in 1904, home to the country's most sought-after prepster, a homegrown, prematurely balding sprinter named Bill Hogenson. On several occasions that year, the nineteen-year-old, sturdy-legged Hogenson—whose muscular calves were nearly as large as his quads—had run a near-world-record sub-10-second 100-yard dash. He also had captured AAU championships in both the 100- and 200-yard sprints. For two years, Chicago, its despised rival Michigan, and Princeton had courted Hogenson for their football squads, even though he had been a mediocre player. The schools were enamored with Hogenson's speed, and felt they could coach him into becoming a solid football player. Stagg also had an ulterior motive for wanting to land Hogenson that was unrelated to his gridiron potential: revenge.

Two years prior, Stagg and President Harper—along with

George Varnell's application to the University of Chicago
was submitted in July 1904. (Varnell family archives)

former Major League Baseball pitcher-turned-businessman Albert
Spalding and real estate magnate Henry Furber—had helped con-
vince the International Olympic Committee to select Chicago as
host of its 1904 games. It worked, yet St. Louis eventually "stole"
the games, so Stagg focused on creating as strong a Chicago Olympics team as possible to help stick it to St. Louis. Keeping the champion sprinter Hogenson at home in Chicago would be a major step
toward achieving that goal.

On July 11, 1904, Stagg won the recruiting battle. Newspapers
reported the story, focusing on Hogenson's speed and track records
while also mentioning his lesser-known Lewis Institute teammate,
hurdler and running back George Varnell, who himself had signed
with Chicago the same day after having been wooed by Michigan
and Wisconsin. The *Detroit Free Press* wrote that Varnell had "won
the hurdles and quarter-mile for Lewis Institute this spring …
[and] also is a football player of ability."[4] The *Chicago Daily Tribune*
wrote, "Varnell, the other Lewis man now at Chicago, is a hurdler
and sprinter and a crack man for a relay team. Besides he has an
enviable record as a half back [sic] on the Lewis football team, and
may be counted on to win a position on the Maroon eleven."[5] The
Oshkosh (Wisconsin) *Daily Northwestern* focused its story on the player

its state school had failed to recruit, Varnell, "… a crack sprinter and all-around athlete [and] one of the fastest quarter-milers in the west [who] has already won a name for himself in football with his work in back of the line."[6]

The Oshkosh article also took a jab at Chicago's ethics and academic standards, mentioning that Stagg recently had convinced school administrators to abolish a "three-week rule" stipulating that athletes who had fallen below academic standards were to be removed from their sports' teams for twenty-one days, during which time they would be given an opportunity to improve their grades and regain eligibility. Doing away with the rule allowed athletes to continue competing while on academic probation. "For several years past," the Wisconsin paper wrote, "Stagg has found his [football] teams demoralized at the end of the first three weeks by half the members receiving notice that they had failed in the work and would no longer be permitted to represent the school."[7]

Those familiar with athletics at Chicago and other major colleges of the day did not need a newspaper article to tell them that education was an afterthought for many athletes. At Chicago during fall quarter 1903, only three of the twenty-three football team members were taking even an average course load. And those who were fully enrolled often failed to complete their classes. That quarter, for example, Chicago's star quarterback Walter Eckersall received no credit in two of his three classes.[8]

It did not appear that George Varnell, University of Chicago matriculate number 29076, was much interested in education, either. He declared history as a major, but also indicated he had taken none of the school's entrance exams. On his application, in the space following the question asking which degree he sought, Varnell had written: "None."

That application was submitted to the registrar's office the same day news of his and Hogenson's signings was reported in regional newspapers. Varnell immediately began morning classes and spent the hot afternoons training on Marshall Field—both for a position on Stagg's loaded football team and also for what was considered a much less significant honor: one of the two dozen spots available on the team the Chicago Athletic Association would take to the St. Louis Olympics. Chicago's track was one on which Varnell had raced several times, including a year earlier in a meet sponsored by the Anti-Cigarette League. There he and the other 149 athletes had been required to sign a pledge to "… promise faithfully to abstain from the use of cigarettes, at least until [they were] 21 years of age."[9] Varnell had to abstain for only six weeks; his twenty-first birthday was that August 10.

Running unattached during the Anti-Cigarette race, Varnell won the 220-yard hurdles, besting by eight yards a competitor from the West Side Y.M.C.A. and the First Regiment Athletic Association's Elmer Eckersall, the older brother of Varnell's future college roommate and teammate, Walter Eckersall.

For six weeks that summer of 1904, Varnell trained under the piercing stare of a suit-and-tie-wearing former New York boxer named Mike "Dad" Butler, who once had coached a fighter named George "The Saginaw Kid" Lavigne to a world championship. Varnell's training consisted of 100-, 200-, and 400-yard repeats, general calisthenics, and broad jumps, all in preparation to race the 200- and 400-meter hurdles, the metric equivalents of the yard-measured events he had dominated at Lewis Institute. His training also included running as a "rabbit" for Hogenson's time trials, oftentimes granted a 4-meter head start. At a practice on August 25, 1904, Varnell was doing exactly that when Hogenson finished a 60-meter run in 6.6 seconds, which bested the world record set at the 1900 Paris Olympics. Later that day, Varnell all but locked down his own spot on the team, trouncing all other hopefuls in trials for both the 200- and 400-meter hurdles.

Following an unseasonably cloudy and chilly morning practice on Friday, August 26—one in which 6-foot, 6-inch, 265-pound Michigan thrower Ralph Rose shattered the world discus record by four feet[10]—Coach Butler pulled his young troops aside to announce his Olympic squad. His roster included Rose; middle-distance runners Frank Verner and Lacey Hearn from Purdue; pole vaulter and

Lewis Institute graduate Charles Dvorak, who was attending the University of Michigan; thrower C.S. Rodman and quarter-miler Thomas Peebles from Illinois; hurdler Thaddeus Shideler from Indiana; and mustachioed Frenchman Albert Corey, a marathoner who a year earlier had taken up residence in Chicago and was thus eligible to compete for a United States team. From the University of Chicago, Butler named Hogenson, the favorite to win at least two gold medals in St. Louis; sprinter Clyde Blair; middle-distance runner Jimmy Lightbody; and hurdler George Varnell.

There was little time for celebration. The next morning, the Chicago athletes boarded a train for the 300-mile trip to St. Louis. The Olympic track and field competition was set to begin in two days.

THE 1904 OLYMPICS WERE well under way when George Varnell and the eleven other Chicago athletes arrived in St. Louis. In fact, the official opening ceremony had taken place more than three months earlier, on May 14, in front of 4,000 people at Francis Field on the Washington University campus. Former Governor David R. Francis, for whom the field was named, was president of both the St. Louis Games and the concurrent World's Fair and had fired the pistol shot that opened the preliminary athletic competition—an interscholastic track meet featuring 136 of Missouri's top high school and club athletes. However, neither that interscholastic meet nor the dozen or so other athletic competitions held over the next six weeks were part of the "official" Olympic Games, which had begun July 1. These preliminary events proved confusing to spectators of the day and future Olympic historians alike.

The May 14 opening was held exactly two weeks after opening day for the entire World's Fair, where a much grander ceremony had taken place. Nearly 200,000 people had congregated in the heart of St. Louis to hear John Philip Sousa's famous band perform the *The Star-Spangled Banner*. Then came a miles-long parade welcoming representatives of sixty-two countries and forty-three of the forty-five American states to the technology-themed Louisiana Purchase Exposition.

The *real* Olympic Games—the ones featuring top athletes from around the world—had opened with a ceremony that was far less grandiose than either of the spring events. Then, Governor Francis had joined the fair's athletic director, James E. Sullivan, and anthropologist Frederick Skiff at the head of a procession of athletes and officials. They walked double-file through the stadium while a band played and gymnasts warmed up in the center of the field.[11]

In retrospect, the modest ritual befitted the disappointing games. As Modern Olympics founder Pierre de Coubertin had feared, getting to St. Louis had proved a problem for many potential competitors. In the end, only twelve countries and 651 athletes paid their two-dollar-per-person fee to come to St. Louis to compete for gold, silver, and bronze medals. Only six of those 651— all archers—were women, and more than 500 of the athletes were from various U.S. club teams, including the twelve from the Chicago Athletic Association. The United States did not have one official national team at the time, as it does today, nor did it hold official Olympic trials. It was up to club teams to choose their athletes and fund their own way to the host site. If there were too many athletes in a particular event, heats were held. If not, it was straight to the finals.

One-hundred forty-two of those Olympians were in St. Louis to compete in the twenty-six track and field events scheduled from August 29 through September 3. In what was perhaps the surest prognostication in sports-forecasting history, the *St. Louis Post-Dispatch* foretold American dominance: "It is not American victory, however, so much as a world victory, so much as a smashing of old records, that we are looking forward to next week. The only question is as to whether American athletes will sweep the board clean. … It is to wear the wreath of fame that adorns the ancient Greek athletes that the best manhood of today will be exerted in the Stadium."[12]

Varnell's first event, the 400-meter hurdles, was not sched-

Archie "The Milwaukee Meteor" Hahn won three gold medals in the 1904 Olympics.
He went on to coach football at several institutions, including Whitman College in
Washington state, where George Varnell refereed many of his team's games. (SDN-
002633B, Chicago Sun-Times/Chicago Daily News collection, Chicago History Museum)

uled until August 31, affording him a few days to acclimate while watching his teammates compete. First among those teammates was his former schoolmate Bill Hogenson, whose 60-meter race on the morning of August 29 opened the track and field portion of the Olympics. Heats were held, and Hogenson easily passed into the finals, where his main competition was expected to be Archie "The Milwaukee Meteor" Hahn, a diminutive twenty-three-year-old from the University of Michigan competing for his hometown Milwaukee Athletic Club. When the race began, Hahn blasted off the line and through the tape in 7 seconds. Hogenson—without his erstwhile rabbit, Varnell—finished two-tenths of a second behind.

Varnell also watched that day as his teammates Frank Waller and Herman Groman finished second and third, respectively, in the 400 meters behind the New York Athletic Club's Harry Hillman. Another thrilling race saw Chicago's stiff-postured Jimmy Light-body bound over wooden hurdles and water obstacles to win the

Thomas Hicks, winner of the 1904 Olympic marathon, received a little help during his race. George Varnell watched the final laps of the 24.85-mile race from inside the Olympic stadium. (Missouri Historical Society)

2,590-meter steeplechase by one second over Ireland's John Daly.

Varnell returned to the grounds the following day to witness what he could of the day's only event, a scandal-filled marathon that ended up being one of the oddest races in Olympic history. Thirty-two runners—a majority of whom never had raced anywhere near the 24.85 miles (the 26.2-mile marathon distance used today was not formally established until 1921) they would be running on the humid ninety-degree day—started the race. It would take them over traffic- and pedestrian-filled dirt streets and paths covered with dust so thick that it caused choking fits. One California runner nearly died when his stomach hemorrhaged due to dust inhalation. There were only two water stations along the route, and eighteen runners dropped out along the way.

The first person to cross the finish line, to the cheers of Varnell and others, was a bricklayer from New York named Fred Lorz, who had finished fifth earlier in the year in the Boston Marathon. Yet Lorz's celebration did not last long; he soon was disqualified after it was discovered he had covered several miles seated inside a support vehicle before reentering the race.

Second-place finisher Thomas Hicks, an English-born brass worker living in Massachusetts and competing for the United States, was awarded the gold, even though his support team had not only propped him up for a portion of the race but also had fed him French brandy and a mixture of egg whites and strychnine a handful of miles from the end. "As Hicks passed the twenty-mile point, his color became ashen pale, and then another tablet of one-sixtieth grain strychnine was administered to him, and two more eggs, besides a sip of brandy," author Charles J.P. Lucas wrote in 1905. Lucas would have known; he was one of Hicks's handlers, riding near him in a car during the historic race. "His entire body," Lucas continued, "was bathed in warm water, including his head, the water having been kept warm along the road by being placed on the boiler of a steam automobile."[13]

Hicks finished in 3:28:53, slow even by the day's standards but valiant considering the conditions. He had lost eight pounds during the race, and was too weak at the finish to accept a special silver trophy purchased by fair president Francis. Albert Corey, the Frenchman competing for Chicago, finished second.

AUGUST 31 WAS "MINING GULCH DAY" at the fair, one in which 10,000 free watermelons were handed out and two couples were married atop a 264-foot-tall observation wheel, the Ferris wheel, that bridge-builder George Ferris Jr. had constructed for the 1893 Chicago World's Fair.

In the Northwest corner of the expo grounds in the fair's Physical Culture zone, near the nursery, dormitories, and an anthropology exhibit, day three of the Olympics track and field portion began at two-thirty in the afternoon on Francis Field. Chicago's Ralph Rose, the hulking, bushy-haired holder of the world shot put record, set an Olympic record with his first throw in that event, only to see his mark bested by the next man up, Wesley Coe of Yale. Coe's mark of 47 feet, 3 inches held up for four tosses, until Rose shattered it and his own world record on his fifth and final attempt, putting the sixteen-pound shot 48 feet, 7 inches. The put was so long, it flew over the marked board and landed on the infield grass.

The second of the day's six events saw sprinters Archie Hahn and Bill Hogenson face off again, this time in the 200-meter finals. Hogenson finished third in the four-man field, thanks mostly to a one-yard penalty he received for a false start, while Hahn won in 21.6 seconds.

George Varnell's 400-meter hurdles race was next. Charles J.P. Lucas wrote that the four-man contest was "second to no other event in importance"[14] in St. Louis because it was an East-versus-West rivalry match between the New York Athletic Club and the Chicago Athletic Association. The presence of the Milwaukee Athletic Club's George Poage was an added attraction. Born in 1880 in Hannibal, Missouri, and raised in La Crosse, Wisconsin, Poage had enrolled in the University of Wisconsin, where he became the first-ever Black American to compete in track there and later the first Black Big Ten Conference champion, an honor he earned in 1904 by winning both the 220-yard and 440-yard hurdles.

Despite the intriguing storylines, the race itself was anticlimactic. Hillman led over each of the 30-inch-high wooden barriers and finished in a world-record time of 53 seconds, although that record was disallowed because he had knocked over a hurdle. Chicago's Frank Waller finished two-tenths of a second back, and Poage took third, becoming the first-ever Black athlete to win an Olympic medal. Just hours after Poage won his bronze, another Black Olympian, Joseph Stadler of Cleveland, won a silver medal by finishing second in the standing high jump.

Poage's achievement was by far the most culturally significant event of the 1904 games. By comparison, Varnell's fourth-place finish—one in which he raced even with the leaders until the fourth hurdle—was but a historical addendum. While at least a few record books note Poage's finishing time of 56.8 seconds, no time for Varnell can be found.

The rest of the third-day highlights included Chicago's Jimmy

Harry Hillman, front left, wins the men's 400-meter hurdles race in the 1904 Olympics. Frank Waller, right, finished second, and George Poage, at left in background, finished third. George Varnell, not pictured, placed fourth. (Missouri Historical Society)

Lightbody outkicking a field of thirteen to win the 800 meters in 1:56, and recent gold medalist Ralph Rose finishing a disappointing sixth in the fifty-six-pound weight throw.

THE SHORT VARNELL appeared to have a better chance at a medal the following day in the finals of the 200-meter hurdles, where he lined up against Hillman, Poage, and two other Americans— Frank Castleman of the Greater New York Irish Athletic Club and Frederick Schule, Poage's teammate from Milwaukee. In the end, Hillman bested Castleman by three-tenths of a second with a time of 24.6 seconds, breaking the Olympic record in the process. Poage had led for a large portion of the race but finished third, earning his second bronze medal in as many days. "The race was one of the prettiest of the day, the first three men crossing the tape in a bunch," one newspaper reported.[15]

Varnell, despite possessing a powerful lower body perfectly suited to the shorter bursts of speed required in the 200-meter dis-

The homestretch of the 1904 Olympic 200-meter hurdles finals, showing runners
Harry Hillman (center of frame), George Poage (second competitor from right),
and Frederick Schule (competitor at right). Hurdlers Frank Castleman and George
Varnell are not in the frame. (Missouri Historical Society)

tance, finished fourth, and Schule came in fifth.

His Olympic events over, Varnell spent the rest of the next day—an off day for competitors—exploring the World's Fair. The day after that found him once again acting as a cheerleader as he watched his teammates. Bill Hogenson finished third in the 100 meters, and Jimmy Lightbody, Frank Verner, and Lacey Hearn swept the 1,500 meters. Thaddeus Shidler finished second in the 110-meter hurdles to Frederick Schule, and Charles Dvorak won the pole vault. Ralph Rose captured his third medal, a silver, in the discus. The team awards ceremony was canceled when Butler and the rest of the Chicago coaches filed a protest over the final scoring, which had allowed the New York Athletic Club to walk off with the coveted Spalding Victory Cup. It took two months, but Chicago's multitiered grievance eventually was rejected.

Varnell and his teammates hopped a train back to Chicago, and the Olympics continued for two and a half more months.

The front and back of a replica of the medal George Varnell and other competitors received for participating in the 1904 Olympics. (Olympic Artifacts)

Swimming and diving took place in the middle of the fairgrounds in manmade, and often-stagnant, United States Life Saving Exhibition Lake. Fencing and boxing were held in the gymnasium; archery, wrestling, and soccer on the stadium field; and golf at a local country club. The Olympics wrapped up November 23, one week before closing ceremonies for the World's Fair. The final Olympic medal count was as lopsided as everyone had predicted: The United States won seventy-eight gold, eighty-two silver, and seventy-nine bronze medals for a total of 239. Germany was second, with thirteen total medals.

The 1904 Olympics marked the first time gold, silver, and bronze medallions were awarded. Many of Varnell's teammates returned home with those round pendants, each stamped with a chiseled male athlete grasping a victory wreath. Varnell left St. Louis with two octagonal copper participation medals featuring a nude, slightly bulky runner in midstride holding a laurel branch in his right hand.

MAROONED

IN THE ADMINISTRATORS' BUDGET SHEETS and in the hearts of
the school's 2,439 students, football was king at the University
of Chicago during the 1904-05 school year. In a year when
seven of the school's eight intercollegiate sports teams lost money,
Chicago's athletic department still finished in the black, thanks to
the massive success of its football program, which earned nearly
$64,000 (approximately $2.1 million in 2022 dollars) on ticket sales
alone for its home games at Marshall Field.[1]

More particularly, Amos Alonzo Stagg was responsible for
that positive budget. In 1892, the university had lured the thirty-
year-old football coach with an offer incentivized by a promise of
full tenure and the newly created titles of associate professor and
director of physical culture and athletics. Stagg's acceptance had
made him the first-ever fully tenured coach in U.S. history.[2] And
despite having to insert himself in the lineup for the first couple sea-

sons due to low player turnout, Stagg had soon built Chicago into a football powerhouse. Though his team's yearly record was padded with wins against high schools, athletic clubs, and smaller regional colleges, the Chicago Maroons had never had a losing season on Stagg's watch, and regularly had defeated top Western Conference opponents Indiana, Illinois, Purdue, and Wisconsin.

Much of that success came from Stagg's innovative coaching philosophy, as well as his focus on recruitment. Oftentimes, Stagg sought verbal commitments from athletes during their sophomore years of high school. Relentless marketing by Stagg and school president William Rainey Harper also had paid dividends, and the faculty, students, and community had become enamored with the Maroons. Home games at Marshall Field regularly drew more than 10,000 fans. Long before the National Football League's Chicago Bears adopted the nickname (as well as the university's wishbone "C" logo the NFL team still uses today), the Maroons were branded as the "Monsters of the Midway," dubbed after a park running through campus.

Beginning in 1903, many were coming to games to see star quarterback Walter Eckersall, a graduate of nearby Hyde Park High School. A childhood fan of Chicago football, Eckersall was a state-record-holding sprinter with a personal best of 10 seconds in the 100-yard dash. Unlike many pure athletes whom football coaches would try to mold into good football players, Eckersall had long been good at that sport, as well. During his senior year, he had led Hyde Park to an undefeated season that culminated in a 105-0 win over Brooklyn (New York) Poly Prep in the unofficial high school national championship game. During his junior year, Eckersall had wowed the Marshall Field crowd, and Coach Stagg, too, with his athleticism as he led his high school team to a surprising 6-0 win over the University of Chicago in an early-season contest.[3] It was that performance, and the subsequent pressure from university administrators after an embarrassing loss to a high school team, that led Stagg to up the ante in his recruitment of Eckersall to a level that today would be subject to sanctions. As legend

George Varnell's teammate, and roommate, at the University
of Chicago, Walter Eckersall, was an All-American quarterback
in 1904, 1905, and 1906. (Missouri Historical Society)

goes, Eckersall first committed to the University of Chicago, but
was then convinced by the University of Michigan to visit its Ann
Arbor campus. When Stagg was tipped off, he showed up at the
Englewood train station on Chicago's south side and yanked Eckersall off the platform.

Competition—as well as possibly the fear of losing his job—
fueled Stagg's passion for Eckersall. There was no more remarkable
football rivalry than Chicago-Michigan; the roots predated the
teams' first official meeting in 1892. Michigan's first-ever football
game, in fact, had been held in the city of Chicago in 1879, and later Michigan had held multiple matchups in town against teams of
select athletes—including many current and former college stars—
who called themselves the Chicago University Club. Those contests
had given Michigan a football foothold in Chicago, allowing it to
lure many of the city's most promising prep athletes 250 miles east
to Ann Arbor.

The founding of the University of Chicago in 1890, and Stagg's arrival two years later, helped Chicago build a recruiting wall around the city, one fortified by Stagg's university-backed recruiting plan, which often included ethically iffy incentives such as free room and board. Stagg's plan—coupled with his affable personality—eventually worked, and after a few startup struggles, the University of Chicago began to hold its own on the field against Michigan. From Stagg's first season in 1892 to his ninth in 1900, in fact, the series between the two schools was nearly split, with Michigan winning five games and Chicago four.

In 1901, however, Michigan recaptured momentum when it hired as coach an experienced thirty-year-old West Virginian named Fielding Yost. Yost's playing experience had been limited to a short stint as a tackle at West Virginia. But his head coaching résumé already included year-long stints, winning seasons all, at Ohio Wesleyan, Nebraska, Kansas, and Stanford, as well as a one-game interim stopover at San Jose State.

Yost's teams almost always dominated. His 1900 Stanford team, for example, outscored opponents 154-20, prompting Michigan's athletic director, Charles Baird, to recruit him. It was perfect timing. Yost, though he had finished his first season with a 7-2-1 record, had been fired by Stanford due to a recently passed rule mandating that all Stanford coaches needed to be alumni. So, in October 1901, Yost signed a one-year, $2,300 (approximately $80,000 in 2022 dollars) contract with Michigan, and also received "… a sum sufficient to cover his traveling expenses to and from Ann Arbor and his living expenses while in the city."[4]

Yost brought to Michigan his hurry-up approach based on a formation Stagg had invented that gave offenses multiple options on every play. Yost perfected the pattern, called the short punt formation, leading area newspapers to dub his dynamic offense "point-a-minute." The coach's tough preseason practice schedule included fourteen-hour days in which players would awaken at seven o'clock in the morning, spend hours studying the rules of the game, take quizzes on what they had learned, and end the day practicing for-

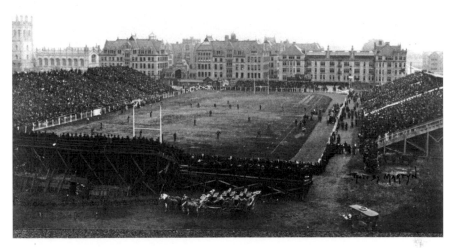

Chicago's historic Marshall Field, shown here October 22, 1904, during a Chicago-Northwestern contest won by Chicago, 32-0. (University of Chicago Library archives)

mations in between training swims in a nearby lake.[5]

Yost's 1901 Michigan team had a solid defense, too, and did not allow a single point as it scored 555 of them in an 11-0 season that included a 22-0 win over the Maroons and a 49-0 victory over his former Stanford squad, the latter coming on January 1, 1902, at Pasadena, California, in the Tournament East-West game, known today as the Rose Bowl. Yost was rewarded with a three-year contract that upped his annual salary to $2,750, and his 1902 and 1903 teams also went undefeated. The 1902 Michigan team beat the Chicago Maroons, 21-0, and the 1903 Michigan team ended Chicago's season with a 28-0 win in front of a record-breaking Marshall Field crowd of 20,000. Stagg had been ill for that 1903 contest, but still coached, "… bundled up in blankets in a closed carriage."[6] Several inches of rain had fallen prior to game time, and Eckersall had played so poorly that he was replaced at quarterback in the second half by one of the team's linemen.

At Chicago, that trend of blowout losses to Michigan stung. Stagg, his boss Harper, the students, alumni, and community at large all had grown frustrated by Michigan's newfound dominance. Stagg was determined to stem the tide. He dedicated the offseason to reviving his program, redoubling efforts to recruit blue-chippers. Along with George Varnell and Bill Hogenson of Chicago's Lewis Institute, Stagg had secured top local recruits Ed Hill and Leo DeTray of North Division High School; Gerry Williamson of East Milwaukee High School; Bill Speidel,* a University of Washington graduate and former UW quarterback attending medical school at Chicago; center Lewis Shearer, another Washington football alumni attending graduate school at Chicago; and a series of other players to compete with his returning starters for spots alongside star quarterback Eckersall.

Such aggressive recruitment put Chicago's athletic program under a national microscope, with many decrying the school's tactics as unethical. In a time when player compensation of any kind, including scholarships, was forbidden, Chicago and other big-time football programs were finding ways to skirt the rules. *Collier's Weekly* magazine lamented, "Western educators who have helplessly watched this campaign place the University of Chicago first among the violators of the trust which rests upon all universities for the conservation of academic ideals."[7] The school's retention of Eckersall, the magazine wrote, was perhaps the most egregious violation ever of the ethics of amateur athletics. "[He] is simply an 'athletic ward' of the University of Chicago, retained under her system of official 'maintenance' as a factor in building her athletic prestige. … Although short three of the minimum number of credits for the admission of the most poorly prepared freshman, Eckersall entered Chicago, and received free tuition during his entire course, with no return except in kicking and tackling ability. … [He] has twice been disqualified by the Chicago faculty for poor academic work, but never during the football season."[8]

---

* Bill Speidel later returned to the University of Washington and played a key role in convincing the school to hire Hiram Conibear. Conibear eventually became a legendary rowing coach and creator of a famous stroke that bears his name. Additionally, Speidel's son, Bill Jr., became a prolific Northwest author and also founded the Seattle Underground Tour, which still is in operation today. The current University of Washington shell house is named in honor of Conibear.

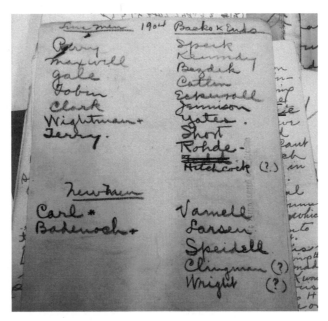

Amos Alonzo Stagg's handwritten notes from 1904 include a mention
of his team's new players. George Varnell was among them. (Cole
Paxton, A.A. Stagg Papers, University of Chicago Library archives)

The *Collier's* article also blasted Chicago's recruitment of De-
Tray, saying the high schooler previously had been offered incentives from two other colleges before "… theatre tickets, dinner parties, and complimentary tickets to Chicago athletic contests were
all employed to turn the boy's attention to Chicago."[9]

According to Stagg's personal notes, contained in more than
300 boxes in the Special Collections Research Center of the University of Chicago Library, some of these recruits never made it
onto the roster—or to the school, for that matter. But George Varnell—to whom no extra incentives were known to have been given
or even needed, considering the once-immense wealth of his late
father—did both. Varnell's name first appears in a column of "New
Men" Stagg penned in cursive on the back of a piece of university
stationery in summer 1904.[10]

In addition to a load of new players, Stagg also introduced

The 1904 University of Chicago football team, which included 158-pound running
back George Varnell, encircled in the bottom row, finished with an 11-1-1 record.
(University of Chicago Library archives)

several tactics prior to the 1904 season. On defense, Stagg wrote
in his notes: "Every man should aim to be in the tackle [box and]
follow the ball like a pack of hounds after a fox."[11] On special teams:
"After catching a kickoff, the man in the center of the field should
not run to the side line but straight down the field."[12] On offense:
A blocker should take out his opponent, then he "… must finish his
play right there. He must not expect to be of any value afterwards
on that particular play. The same is true when interfering on a run
when our runner gets loose. A good method is to dive sideways at
the man's knees."[13]

In spite of a daunting upcoming season, Stagg's optimism grew
once this new squad hit the practice field. *The Chicago Inter Ocean*
newspaper wrote, "No Western team has ever attempted so hard
a schedule as that outlined for the Chicago 1904 team."[14] Games
were booked against all other members of the "big nine" Western
Conference, except Minnesota. The first four games of the 1904

season were not among those difficult ones, however. Stagg's theory was that by beginning each season with lesser opponents, his players could get some extra practice while simultaneously rallying and exciting the fan base with easy victories. It is a scheduling trend many major colleges follow to this day.

Maroons practices were almost as intense as games. During one on September 14, 1904, three days before the team's first game against Lombard College, three Maroons were injured—by the school's tackling dummy. The 158-pound Varnell was among those three, losing a slice of his right ear during one collision. After that practice, Stagg said he believed his team could win the Western Conference. The team responded on September 17 with a 40-5 home victory over Lombard, a small school from Galesburg, Illinois. Lombard's only points came at the end of the game with Chicago backups on the field. Then, after one of the Chicago reserves fumbled, a Lombard player scooped up the ball and ran the length of the field for a touchdown.[*]

After the victory, a confident Stagg praised his backfield of Eckersall, DeTray, and the "brilliant"[15] Varnell. But Stagg's self-belief faded the following week after a particularly poor practice. An article in *The Minneapolis Journal* headlined "Stagg gives up hope of winning" quoted the coach as saying, "With the material now on hand, Chicago cannot be a factor in the fight for the western football championship this fall. I am greatly disappointed in the showing made by the line men in the Lombard game Saturday, and unless some new forwards with experience arrive soon, we will have a poor team."[16] The same article said Stagg was "… well pleased with the way the back fielders got into it … DeTray's work was certainly fine, and Varnell, Hogenson, and Hayes did themselves credit, but the line was a failure. … I expect four good [line]men to report this week, and my hopes to a large extent depend on the caliber they show."[17]

---

[*] During Varnell's playing days, touchdowns were worth 5 points, field goals were worth 4 points, conversions were worth 1 point, and safeties were worth 2 points.

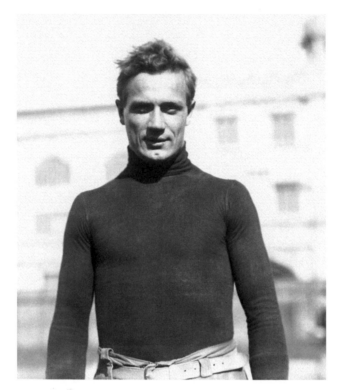

George Varnell during his playing days at the University of Chicago. (Chicago Daily News Collection, Chicago History Museum: SDN-002655)

The Maroons bounced back. The following afternoon, in front of 600 Marshall Field fans, the team trounced Englewood High School, 72-0, in a hastily scheduled Wednesday game that consisted of a twenty-minute first half and a ten-minute second half. "About the only practice the varsity got was in running," *The Chicago Inter Ocean* reported, "and the Maroon backs ought to have much better wind and endurance from this time forth."[18] Varnell scored six touchdowns in the first half, his two longest on off-tackle runs of forty and sixty-five yards. "The Lewis Institute lad showed exceptional cleverness on his feet, sidestepping and dodging much after the fashion of the famous [former Maroons All-American full-back Clarence] Hirschberger [sic]," *The Chicago Inter Ocean* reported.

George Varnell ran for three touchdowns in this October 1, 1904, game against Indiana at Marshall Field in Chicago. The Maroons won, 56-0. (SDN-002282, Chicago Sun-Times/Chicago Daily News collection, Chicago History Museum)

"[Varnell] was weak, however, in interfering for the other runners, and has much to learn in this respect."[19] University of Washington transfer Speidel and a 22-year-old newcomer from Prague named Hugo Bezdek also scored touchdowns for Chicago.

That Saturday, the Maroons beat Lawrence University, 29-0, at Marshall Field in a sloppy game that again left Stagg disappointed in his linemen yet pleased with the backfield play of Eckersall, Bezdek, Varnell, and Hogenson. Varnell had a short touchdown run in the second half, while Hogenson scored another in his first game for the Maroons.

The following week brought North Division High School to Marshall Field for a rainy and windy midweek contest in front of 500 fans. Though they outweighed their opponents by an average of twenty pounds per man, the sloppy Maroons squad mustered just three touchdowns for an 18-0 win. Varnell was held without a touchdown for the first time in the season, though his running— if not his blocking—did help set up all three of the scores of his backfield mates. "Varnell was as clever on his feet as in the earlier games,"[20] *The Chicago Inter Ocean* reported.

The North Division game was the last warm-up for Stagg's squad before conference play. The Western Conference, at the time, was one of college football's five major divisions, along with The

Eastern Independent (which included the likes of Pennsylvania, Princeton, Navy, and Notre Dame), The Northeast Independent (featuring Harvard, Dartmouth, Yale, and Army), The Southern Independent (with Alabama, Georgetown, Virginia, and Auburn), and The Western Independent (led by Colorado, Kansas, Texas, and Nebraska).

The nine-team Western Conference was comprised of Chicago, Michigan, Minnesota, Illinois, Northwestern, Wisconsin, Purdue, Iowa, and Indiana. The quality of the conference's football had come a long way in the past decade, thanks to Stagg's efforts at Chicago, Yost's work at Michigan, and the hiring of former Yale player Henry Williams at Minnesota. Since his hiring in 1900, Williams's squads had lost only three games and had twice tied for first place. In 1904, national opinion was divided on whether the big three of the Western Conference could stand toe to toe with the nation's top teams in the east, but few argued that the quality of western football was at least comparable to what was being played at those schools. For his part, Stagg, the former Yale all-American, believed western football was "… so far ahead of the East in speed, variety and originality of attack, [because] the game is much more open and dashing here."[21] Eastern football, by contrast, was considered a more technically proficient style of play.

Chicago's first conference game came October 1 against an Indiana team that was neither open and dashing nor technically proficient. Under veteran coach James Horne, the Hoosiers had won half their games the previous year, but also had been blown out by both Michigan and Chicago by a combined score of 85-0.

Stagg's game preparation was hindered by an off-field incident that drew attention from newspapers across the country. Earlier in the season, a lineman named Bobby Maxwell had left Chicago to play football at Swarthmore College in Pennsylvania, after which time Maxwell's mother claimed that her son had done so because Stagg had mistreated him. Stagg admitted that he had denied Maxwell free board when the player had asked for it, but added, "The trouble rests with 'Max' himself, who, despite his great bulk, is still more of a boy than a man."[22]

No negative effects of the distraction were evident that Saturday when the home team hit the field, as the Maroons took an early lead and piled it on from there, winning 56-0. Varnell ran for three touchdowns, including an 80-yarder in the second half that newspapers reported as the game's offensive highlight. The game also marked the end of Varnell's regular playing time for the season. Varnell left late in the game, badly bruised from a series of hard hits.[23] He briefly played the following week in his team's 20-0 home win against Purdue, spelling Hogenson during the first half until he twisted his ankle and returned to the bench. That injury left him on the sidelines during the following week's 39-0 win against Iowa, although Varnell had practiced sparingly that week, one in which Stagg introduced his players to one of his lesser-known innovations: white-painted footballs so his team could continue to practice after dark when "spies" from other teams had left the practice area.[24]

Varnell also did not play in his team's 32-0 win over Northwestern nor in its 6-6 tie with Illinois. He did play sparingly in the second half of a 68-0 win over Texas on November 5, but did not see action in either his team's hard-fought 22-12 loss at Michigan on November 12 in front of 13,500 fans, nor during the final game of the season, an 18-11 home win over Wisconsin on November 24.

The Chicago Maroons finished the 1904 season with a record of 10-1-1, good for third place in the Western Conference behind undefeated co-champions Michigan and Minnesota. Michigan was awarded a share of the national championship, splitting the title with the University of Pennsylvania.

Varnell's battered body had healed enough by early 1905 to allow him to compete as planned for the Maroons's swimming, indoor track, water polo, and baseball teams. But his grades never allowed him to do so. That January, Varnell was among several "athletic flunkers"[25] whose poor classroom work had left them ineligible. A newspaper article later in the month said the loss of Varnell, as well as sprinter Clyde Blair, had left the 1905 track team "badly crippled."[26] A February story in *The Chicago Inter Ocean* on

The 1905 Chicago Athletic Association track team included several noteworthy athletes.
George Varnell, circled at bottom left, was among them, as were his Olympic teammates
Clyde Blair (second row, second from left), Jimmy Lightbody (second row, center),
Frank Verner (third row, far left), Ralph Rose (top row, center), and Coach Mike "Dad"
Butler (second row in bowtie). (The Chicago Inter Ocean)

North Division High School's dominating win over the University of Chicago's swim team attributed the loss to the absence of Chicago's three best swimmers. Varnell was one of them.[27]

Varnell still had an itch to compete. Along with four other Maroon athletes—including Blair, middle-distance runners Jimmy Lightbody and Herman Groman, and sprinter Bill Hogenson—he began training with the Chicago Athletic Association with the intention of competing in an important March track meet hosted by the First Regiment Athletic Association. But the announced participation of Varnell and the others caused a rift between the athletic association and the university, whose policy was to not allow its athletes to compete for outside organizations as long as they were enrolled at the school. The situation played out in the newspapers, until the five Chicago men withdrew from the competition.

Although the *Chicago Daily Tribune* had reported at the end of

January that Varnell still was regularly enrolled at the university and that he had every intention of further participating on its sports teams, there are no records of him competing for the Maroons after his brief appearance in the football game against Texas the previous November.

For a while, Varnell remained active with his fraternity, Chi Psi, whose official records listed him as set to graduate, shortly before his twenty-sixth birthday, with the class of 1908. Varnell attended the twentieth annual banquet of Chi Psi's alumni association on January 14, 1905, at the Hamilton Club, where he sang fraternity songs, dined on everything from "salted almonds to café noir," and gave a toast discussing his first impressions of the fraternity.[28] Varnell left the university shortly thereafter, planning to return in the fall. Chi Psi, however, did not wait for him, and "after prolonged consideration and advice from the alumni" expelled him that June.[29]

Varnell remained in Chicago, at home with his family, for a few months after leaving the university. No longer constrained by the school's competition rules, he resumed competing as a hurdler for the Chicago Athletic Association and attended meets as far away as Portland, Oregon, proudly sporting the team's cherry circle tank top while doing so. He defeated all comers in the low hurdles, including that year's Western Conference champion, Marc Catlin of Chicago.

But when midfall rolled around, Varnell did not return to the university. He never took the field for that fall's undefeated Chicago Maroons football team, which handed Michigan its first loss in five years and won a national championship. Instead, Varnell was some 400 miles to the south of Chicago, still pursuing his passion for sports—and now also pursuing love.

5

HIS NEW KENTUCKY HOME

THE DALLAS MORNING NEWS painted Kentucky University's November 1905 win over the University of Texas as a David-versus-Goliath clash, one in which the smaller and less experienced Texas boys employed a "never-die spirit" against a team of "thoroughly trained" Kentucky men that only squeaked out a win thanks to a fortuitous bounce of a tipped ball.[1]

But according to the *Lexington* (Kentucky) *Leader*, whose story was based on a telegram from Austin, Kentucky University's 6-0 victory never was in doubt. The team, it reported, had simply worked the outclassed Texans "to a frazzle."[2]

Their narratives dramatically differed, yet both papers agreed that the star of the game, the man who scored the winning touchdown and kicked the subsequent extra point, was Kentucky University fullback George Varnell. "The Kentucky line had charged and Varnell, ahead of the mass, grabbed the ball and ran the distance for a touchdown,"[3] explained the Dallas paper. The *Leader's* account was more theatrical: "While the lines were tied up in a fierce scrimmage Varnell, who got the ball and tucked it under his arm, darted round the end like a cyclone and succeeded in getting past the Texas tackle, carrying the ball home. Even the Texas rooters cheered this remarkable feat."[4]

Kentucky University supporters who had traveled to Texas for the Friday-evening game took to the Austin streets to celebrate, marching two by two and chanting through megaphones. "Ordinarily such proceedings would have been construed as a 'disturbance,'" the *Leader* wrote, "but the spirit of good feeling ... had taken possession of the guardians of peace and the boys were not [harmed] in any way."[5] Varnell and his teammates certainly felt harmed. The bout had been a brutal one, in which one Kentucky player had three teeth knocked out. He, and the rest of the KU Pioneers, recovered aboard a southbound Missouri-Kansas-Texas Railroad car to Dallas for the following night's game against Texas A&M. The "spirit of good feeling" followed Varnell and his teammates, as they scored a 29-6 victory over Texas A&M, and a 6-0 win two days later against the University of Arkansas in Little Rock. Three football games in four days.

More than 300 fans greeted the Kentucky University Pioneers when their train arrived home in Lexington shortly before noon on November 15. Each player made his way through the cheering crowd, shaking hands, and accepting hugs from family and from strangers. They rode to the school's Morrison Chapel in cars festooned with crimson streamers. There, Alfred Fairhurst, a Kentucky University science professor, kicked things off:

> "[T]here are enough of these heroes present to give you all the inspiration you need. They have been to Texas ... It is part of the saddest history of the world that its best men have been stoned. The better the man the more stones. Even St. Paul was stoned, and now we must have it chronicled that down in Texas stones were thrown at the KU football team, but we welcome

them home, thankful that no heads are broken."[6]

Fairhurst concluded his speech by inviting the players to an oyster dinner.

Judge Lyman Chalkley, dean of KU's law school and another strong athletic booster, was up next:

> "I say hurrah for Kentucky University, I say hurrah for the Kentucky University football team, I say hurrah for Kelley, I say hurrah for Wallace, I say hurrah for Varnell, I say hurrah for each man on the team. These men went to fight our battles and won and now we shall win. We have a right to win. An unjust and unfounded attack has been made upon them and upon us and we have attacked no one."[7]

Varnell—the team's twenty-three-year-old newcomer—was at the center of the attacks to which Fairhurst and Chalkley referred. They stemmed from a years-long controversy that had dominated newspaper headlines and would become a key subject in many books, including Gregory Kent Stanley's *Before Big Blue: Sports at the University of Kentucky 1880-1940*. An entire chapter of Stanley's 1996 book is, in fact, dedicated to that controversy—universities' use of "ringers," semi-professional athletes who were at best part-time students.

In the early twentieth century, as the financial benefits from football's popularity became apparent, the ringer debate had become a hot-button issue. Lexington's two major teams, Kentucky University and Kentucky State College, each had accused the other of padding their rosters by recruiting seasoned players. The annual Thanksgiving Day game between the two schools had become a big-money event, one in which wagers were high and thousands attended, paying $1.25 for a ticket and fifty more cents to park their carriage.[8] An intense bitterness developed between the schools' administrators, and player-eligibility protests were common prior to—and even after—the games. The *Lexington Herald's* letters to the editor section was abuzz with the controversy.

Rhetoric between the two schools, as well as among other Kentucky colleges, had remained high as the 1905 rivalry game approached. Early in game week, the lightly regarded Kentucky Intercollegiate Athletic Association met with representatives of four state schools on the subject of ringers. A specific discussion about the eligibility of KU's Varnell was high on the agenda. Professor A.H. Throckmorton, dean of Central Kentucky University's law school, opened the meeting by claiming Varnell was ineligible to play football because he had just entered KU at the end of October. Throckmorton then produced a letter from the University of Chicago stating that Varnell had attended school there the previous year. A vote was taken, and Varnell was retroactively declared ineligible to have participated in the November 4 game against Central Kentucky University, a 34-0 Kentucky University win. It was a game in which the *Lexington Herald* had reported, "Varnell, the Law School Man, played a beautiful game at right half back [sic]. He is the best 'fighter' in the K.U. camp, and it always required several C.U. men to down him."[9]

Later in the week, Kentucky State College sent Kentucky University a telegraphed ultimatum with a three-hour deadline: Unless Varnell and another alleged ringer, a student named Wallace, were removed from the lineup, the Thanksgiving Day game was off. Kentucky University refused the offer, instead accusing State College of using ringers of its own. The game was canceled; the saga continued.

Two days before Thanksgiving, the *Lexington Leader* dedicated its second page to the subject. The coverage included a lengthy take from State College's football coach, F.E. Schacht, and the reprinting of a letter-writing battle between Central University's Throckmorton and KU's Chalkley. Throckmorton fired the first shot:

Dear sir: If you will kindly furnish me the following information in regard to Mr. Varnell, who played in the foot ball game against Central University November 4, I shall be obliged and will appreciate the courtesy: 1. When did Mr. Varnell begin work in the University or in the Law School? 2. Where did he come from and what school did he attend last? 3. Is he a bona fide student or is he simply making a pretense of attending Law School in order to play on the foot ball team?[10]

Chalkley responded:

> My Dear Sir: … I take pleasure in furnishing you the following information: 1. Mr. Varnell matriculated in Kentucky University, in the Law College, on October 31 last, and entered upon his duties as such student immediately. … 2. He matriculated from Chicago. I do not know what school he attended last. … 3. I have had no reason to suspect that Mr. Varnell is simply making a pretense of attending the Law School in order to play on the foot ball team until your inquiry raised the question, and I do not believe it.[11]

Chalkley continued, pointing out that Varnell had been initiated into KU's Pi Kappa Alpha fraternity, and that all indications were that he indeed was a legitimate student. The answer did not appease Throckmorton, who wrote:

> I was led to make inquiry of you in regard to Mr. Varnell because I had never heard of him before he appeared in the game at Lexington and upon making inquiry, was informed that he was a "ringer" recently imported from Chicago. … From what I have already learned, there seems to be no doubt that he is a "ringer" and the only remaining question is to be able to prove it. … I trust that you may be able to keep the K.U. Law School free from these athletic "ringers." You will find your task no easy one, however. Ever since I have been in Kentucky, "ringers" have openly and shamelessly played on the K.U. teams …[12]

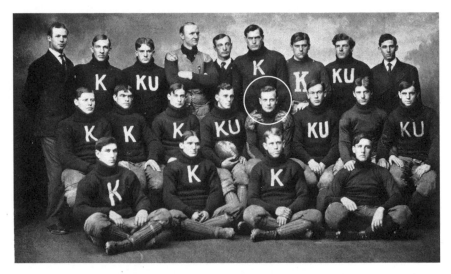

*Despite spending much of the season at the center of controversy, fullback
George Varnell, circled in the center row, led the 1905 Kentucky University
Pioneers to a 7-0-3 record. (Transylvania University)*

KU's football team concluded its 1905 season at home on
Thanksgiving—not against State College, but against Ohio Wesleyan College in a hastily scheduled game. Snow fell throughout,
but the Pioneers plowed their way to a 40-0 victory in front of 2,500
fans to finish the season undefeated, with three ties, at 7-0-3. Varnell scored the game's first touchdown and had several runs greater
than ten yards. The *Lexington Leader* reported, "Varnell was in the
game at every moment, in the middle of every scrimmage, plunging
into every interference, snapping the ball and going down the field
like a cyclone, with a band of Ohioans in his wake."[13] That same
day, Varnell's former squad in Chicago took part in what would
become known as "The Game of the Century," defeating Michigan
for the first time in five years to finish the season 11-0 en route to its
first national championship.

Kentucky University (known today as Transylvania University) soon withdrew from the Kentucky Intercollegiate Athletic Association, and the Thanksgiving Day rivalry between it and State
College (now the University of Kentucky) ended for good. The bat-

tle over ringers soon led to dramatic changes in the eligibility requirements for college athletes across the rest of the United States.

FOLLOWING THE SEASON, at least one member of the KU football
team—perhaps one of the ringers—immediately left school. However, Varnell and Wallace, the school's most controversial players,
remained enrolled through December. By that point, Varnell had
become something of a socialite in Lexington, a bustling city of
30,000. In December, he attended a Spanish- and holiday-themed
masquerade ball hosted by the Girls' German Club. Among the
hundreds of costumed attendees was Varnell's friend, a famous
jockey named Lucien Lyne, who was less than six months away
from winning the Belmont Stakes aboard a three-year-old colt
named Burgomaster.

After the party, rather than hopping a train to Chicago to be
with family, Varnell spent the holidays at Lyne's home near Brannon,
Kentucky. In January, he and Lyne attended a housewarming party
in Lexington, prior to which the pair and a few friends gathered at
the home of Katherine "Kate" Emmal, a student and choir member
at a private Catholic school in Lexington, Campbell-Hagerman
College.

Town football hero though he might have been, Varnell had
not come to Lexington chiefly for sport. Kate Emmal was the main
reason. The two had met in Chicago, where Emmal's father, Joseph Burt Emmal, was an executive with the famous H.H. Kohlsaat Bakery Company, and her mother, Annie Prewitt Emmal, was
a member of the Daughters of the American Revolution. When
Kate chose Lexington—a city where her grandfather, W.B. Emmal, was a prominent banker—as her college destination, Varnell
had followed.

After the housewarming party, Varnell battled an unspecified
illness that left him housebound for days. He was back out on the
town again at the end of January 1906, though, going stag with
several Kentucky University athletes to a cotillion hosted by the

Lexington German Club. In mid-February, he spent one Friday evening at an informal dinner with a few friends, then he traveled to Wheeling, West Virginia, to stay a few days with his brother, Claude, who by then was a part owner of a corporation that dabbled in the buying and selling of natural resources, as well as in horse racing and minor league baseball. In Wheeling, Claude Varnell's company was notorious for running the Wheeling Turf Exchange, a gambling resort similar to what his and George's father, Harry, had operated in Chicago. Also similar to what happened to his father, Claude Varnell had his gaming house raided on several occasions, and was arrested for operating illegally. Once, in April 1910, a police raid at Claude Varnell's parlor resulted in thirty-two arrests.

Upon his return to Lexington, George Varnell was a guest in Lucien Lyne's private box at the opera house for one of the *Lexington Herald's* "events of the week," a play called *A Night in Bohemia*.[14] The next month, George and Kate became regulars at Lyne's house and attended a dance hosted by Varnell's fraternity. The following day, the couple attended an evening affair hosted at a Campbell-Hagerman sorority house, where the "membership of very charming and popular girls" served "ices, cakes, bonbons, all in lavender and white, and salted almonds."[15]

Varnell kept one foot in the affairs of his hometown. In February, he signed a contract to play shortstop that summer for the Chicago Spaldings, a semi-pro baseball team managed by Bob Welch. *The Chicago Inter Ocean* called the club "as strong as any team ever wearing semi-pro colors."[16] Varnell's teammates were to include a German-born, former Major League pitcher named Rudolph Charles "Skel" Roach, who, the previous season, had coached at the University of Michigan. Roach's contract with the Spaldings was unique. It called for him to pitch only on Sundays and holidays, freeing him to play for another team during the rest of the week. Also on the roster was outfielder Roy Clark, who previously had a short stint in the majors with the New York Giants.

Like Roach, Varnell played only intermittently for the Spaldings that season, often choosing to skip games and remain in Lexington with Kate. In April, he captained and played on a basketball team that was hand-picked to challenge the Young Men's Christian Association champions, and he traveled with Kentucky University's baseball team to Millersburg to umpire a game against the Millersburg Military Institute.

On May 27, 1906, George and Kate were among the 300 who attended Phi Delta Theta fraternity's year-end affair at the Merrick Lodge in Lexington, all dancing to the sounds of Saxton & Trost's popular orchestra. The crowd in the ornately decorated, blue-and-white-themed room included guests from across the country. Three days later, Varnell attended Kate's college graduation from Campbell-Hagerman. He then headed southeast to Kentucky's Breathitt County, about 100 miles from Lexington, for his summer job logging in the Appalachian Mountains, where the massive stands of ash, cherry, and oak were being harvested at record pace by lumber companies that already had depleted many of America's northern forests.

He frequently visited Kate in Lexington. In late July, the couple attended a luncheon at the country home of a local businessman with Howard Guyn, a former Kentucky University basketball star who recently had signed a baseball contract with the Cincinnati Reds.[17]

The popular young couple's next newspaper-worthy appearance came about a month later, on August 17, and this time it was front-page news in the *Lexington Leader* under the headline, "Surprise." Three hours before the late edition of the daily paper had gone to press, George and Kate had wed in a short ceremony in a judge's office in the Lexington suburb of Nicholasville. No one from either family attended or knew about the plans. The article was quick to point this out: "The above news is quite a surprise to family and friends here, as they were not told beforehand of the plan of the couple to be married. The bride was in Jessamine County visiting Mr. and Mrs. Warren Fieber, and Mr. Varnell, having come to Lexington last night from the Kentucky mountains and

SURPRISE

To Lexington People is Wedding of Miss Emmal and George Varnell.

[Special to the Leader.]

NICHOLASVILLE, Aug. 17.—The marriage of Miss Katherine Emmal of Lexington and Mr. George Varnell of Chicago took place in Nicholasville to-day at 2 o'clock p. m. Judge Phillps performed the marriage ceremony in his office and the couple are with friends in the country.

A SURPRISE HERE.

The above news is quite a surprise to family and friends here, as they were not told beforehand of the plan of the couple to be married. The bride was in Jessamine county visiting Mr. and Mrs. Warren Fleber, and Mr. Varnell, having come to Lexington last night from the Kentucky mountains and finding that she was there, went to Nicholasville to see her, and the marriage was solemnized today.

Mr. and Mrs. Burt Emmal are the parents of the bride and she is their only child. She was graduated in June from Campbell-Hagerman College and is an unusually charming and talented girl.

Mr. Varnell came from Chicago last fall to be on the foot ball team of Kentucky University and matriculated in the Department of Law.

During the summer he has been engaged in business with a lumber firm in Breathitt county, Kentucky. He belongs to a prominent Chicago family.

The headline in the August 17, 1906, Lexington Leader said it all. (Lexington Leader)

finding that she was there, went to Nicholasville to see her, and the marriage was solemnized today."[18] The article characterized Kate as "an unusually charming and talented girl,"[19] and pointed out that the groom "belongs to a prominent Chicago family."[20]

The Varnells honeymooned in the country, then George returned to the woods. Kate remained in Lexington in her family home, frequently visiting her husband at the logging camp and staying there for as long as two weeks at a time. George returned to Lexington on weekends, and the couple twice traveled to Chicago to visit his family.

Near the end of the summer, the Varnells decided to move to Cincinnati, Ohio, the following spring. That October, George began refereeing college basketball and football games, including those of his onetime adversary, Kentucky State College. He also briefly worked as an unpaid assistant football coach at that school. Apparently, amends had been made.

As the new year arrived, George's pattern of spending weekdays at work in the mountains and weekends with Kate in the city continued. In Lexington, George refereed college basketball games during the day, and then attended various social functions with

Kate at night. The arrangement worked for a while, but on the last day of June 1907, a subtle, one-sentence sign of possible trouble appeared, buried in the society pages of the *Lexington Herald*: "Mrs. George Varnell leaves soon to spend the summer in St. Louis [where her parents recently had relocated]."[21]

Kate Varnell went to St. Louis and did not return to Lexington when the summer was over because—save for her grandfather, an aunt, and some cousins—there was no one for her to return to. No longer was her husband a couple hours away working in the Appalachians. When she headed west, he had, too, albeit nearly 2,000 miles farther, to set up a new life in an area of the country he had visited only once, but one he would call home for the rest of his days.

6

AS SEEN IN SPOKANE

"**T**HE CITY IS DOOMED,"[1] read the *Seattle Post-Intelligencer* on August 5, 1889, one day after a fire in Spokane Falls destroyed thirty-two square blocks and caused millions of dollars of damage to that city of 17,000. The fire that had begun on the third floor of a downtown restaurant and boarding house had feasted on warm summer-evening winds and cheap wooden construction before sputtering out hours later as it reached the Spokane River.

It was easy to see why the *Post-Intelligencer* was so pessimistic. Seattle, just two months prior, had experienced a historic blaze of its own that leveled most of its business district and much of its waterfront. Many reports out of Spokane Falls—some later proved inaccurate—were calamity-filled: A man leaped to his death from a third-story window; a woman died after jumping from the second floor of another building; a dozen corner-lot buildings were blown

Spokane Falls, Washington, became a tent city in 1889, as businesses rebuilt following a major downtown fire on August 4. (Spokane Public Library Northwest Room)

up by dynamite to halt the fire's progress; martial law was declared, and the National Guard was brought in to secure banks and other burned-out businesses.

Spokane Falls doomed? It sure looked like it.

But the residents of Spokane Falls did not feel that way. They rallied and rebuilt, and able-bodied men who failed to pitch in were forced to leave the city. Within days, a new burg was created, one full of white canvas tents built with material secured from Portland, Oregon. Tents that "… quickly began to line the streets, giving the appearance of a war zone. Nearly every type of business enterprise, including about a dozen selling alcohol and offering gambling options, was represented."[2] Donations came from across the United States, and insurance payments helped, too: More than half of the destroyed structures had been protected by a policy. In some ways, the fire had been a blessing, helping to erase the pioneer-town mindset of Spokane Falls and replacing it with a more modern mentality and direction.

The fire alarms of August 4, 1889, proved less a death knell and more a signal of rebirth. Construction soon began on a new downtown full of grand buildings of stone and brick, paid for in part by those insurance monies and also by Dutch investors. Spokane Falls's population grew to an all-time high of 19,222 the following year, and was up more than 5,000 percent from the 356 people who had resided there ten years prior. The city continued growing and in 1891 reincorporated and dropped the "Falls" from its name. By the turn of the twentieth century, some 36,000 people called Spokane home, and the Inland Empire city showed no signs of slowing its growth. The expansion of the Spokane River-driven Washington Water Power Company had helped connect Spokane to surrounding areas, including to mineral-rich Northern Idaho and the fertile-soiled farms elsewhere in the Inland Northwest. The area's thriving timber industry and the arrival of several railroads helped Spokane swell to a population of more than 100,000 by 1910. The "Imperial City"—as promoters came to call the largest burg between Seattle and Minneapolis—became home to dozens of homegrown millionaires, fortune seekers from across the United States, and working-class immigrants from China, Germany, Scandinavia, and Italy. The Children of the Sun—the meaning of "Spokane" in the local Indian tribe's native language—had risen.

THE SPOKANE AMATEUR ATHLETIC CLUB was one of many downtown organizations benefiting from the surge in population and prestige following The Great Fire, as the disaster had become known. Formed in 1892 as the Spokane Wheel Club by a group of fifteen cyclists, the club had changed its name six years later, when it merged with a billiards club. Within two months, membership grew from forty to more than 400. Bicycling and billiards were the club's bedrock, and football was played there, but the still-controversial sport of boxing quickly became its bread and butter. In an average month, unsanctioned "smoker" matches featuring popular fighters of the day would bring in more than $400 ($13,000 in 2022 dollars) in revenue. Often, the bouts were mismatches, and the fighters were poorly paid—five dollars per boxer per match would not be out of the ordinary. "Who's going to turn down the athletic club for robbing moneyless, game lads who go on just because they are broke and need the money?"[3] *The Spokane Press* once asked.

By 1902, the club had more than 700 members and $30,000

*The Spokane Amateur Athletic Club, located at the corner of
Main and Monroe streets, was designed by architect Albert Held
and built in 1904. (Spokane Public Library Northwest Room)*

in assets, some $12,000 of which was the value of land it owned
near the Spokane River at the corner of Main Avenue and Monroe Street. In 1903, as the number of members—many of whom
had paid $150 for a lifetime membership—approached 1,000, club
leaders decided it was time to build a facility on that land and en-
listed club member and renowned local architect Albert Held to
draw up plans. A ruddy-complected University of Minnesota graduate, Held had relocated to Spokane shortly after The Great Fire
in response to a call for architects. He was a member of the Spokane Realty Company and one of Spokane's most gifted designers,
responsible for some of the city's best commercial, municipal, and
residential buildings.

The Spokane Amateur Athletic Club was to be another of the
architect's masterpieces. Such a great deal it was, that when President Theodore Roosevelt visited Spokane on May 26, 1903, the
building's groundbreaking ceremony was on his agenda (though
the president ultimately did not attend the event due to a scheduling issue).

The river-facing, three-story building opened its doors in summer 1904. It cost $100,000 ($3.3 million in 2022 dollars), and in-

cluded a bowling alley, billiard room, and a two-story gymnasium. On the eve of the building's VIP-only opening, *The Spokane Press* reported, "The average young man in this century is inclined to be as flighty as the affections of a summer girl, but give him something to take up his time and attention like the new [club], and he settles down into a steady young man. ... [The club] is the greatest institution in the west. The influences surrounding a member are such as to make a better citizen of him."[4]

The Spokane Amateur Athletic Club's extravagance helped lay to rest a longtime inner-club debate that often had resulted in uprisings and, occasionally, upheaval. Should the club continue to focus solely on recreation for local well-to-do families or strive to field competitive sporting teams that would compete against other regional clubs and thereby bring in further revenue? The latter approach won out. The club began recruiting athletes from across the country to compete on its football, baseball, and track teams.

For an almost-twenty-five-year-old former Olympian and major university football star looking to keep one foot planted in the soft turf of his glory days while the other foot pointed toward the paved streets of adulthood, the chance to again play competitive football was irresistible. When club leadership reached out to George Varnell in Kentucky—his specific connection with club leaders is unknown—to ask him to come to Spokane, his answer was a resounding yes.

Varnell's arrival on July 22, 1907, earned the largest headline of *The Spokane Daily Chronicle*'s sports section, and the accompanying story touted his accomplishments at the University of Chicago and as an assistant coach at Kentucky University, his talent as a baseball infielder, and his appearance in the 1904 Olympics. The article also mentioned the potential for Varnell to become coach of the Spokane Amateur Athletic Club's football team: "[Varnell] stated that while club football was far different from college work, he would not be averse to taking charge of the team if it could be arranged so he could also play with the team while coaching."[5]

Less than a week later, the newspaper ran a large photo of

Varnell, natty in suit and tie, in a story previewing the Spokane Amateur Athletic Club's baseball game against the Spokane Country Club. It was to be played at Recreation Park, home of both the first grass infield in Spokane history and also of the Spokane Indians minor league team. Shortstop Varnell, the story said, "… was considered the most clever that ever took their position behind the pitcher in [Chicago]."[6] Varnell went 5-for-7 with three triples in a 28-8 win, displaying "… speed on the bases such as rarely been shown on a local diamond."[7] Throughout the rest of the summer, Varnell played second base in the semi-pro Trolley League, a circuit that included teams from three small Whitman County, Washington, towns—Rosalia, Palouse, and Colfax—as well as from Moscow, Idaho.

The club's committee liked what it saw in Varnell both on the field and off. On August 8, 1907, the group recommended to its board of directors that Varnell be appointed physical director in charge of all athletics. But two days later, the club announced it would divide those athletics into three sectors: team sports, which Varnell would lead; boxing, to be led by a fighter named George Douglas; and general sports, a department that included the club's wrestling team, to be headed by Cisco Bullivant, who already was, in essence, the club's athletic director. Then, at a special meeting on the afternoon of August 15, the board again reversed course and decided to name Varnell physical director, effective immediately. Said the board's vice president, M.G. Martindale: "Mr. Varnell comes to us with the highest possible recommendations and seems to be just what the club needs."[8] Meanwhile, the board named Bullivant—who was spending the summer recreating in Hope, Idaho—chairman of the athletic committee. Douglas was not mentioned.

Varnell immediately went to work, writing the athletic directors at the University of Idaho, the University of Washington, and Washington State College to request football games that fall. He also shifted Spokane Amateur Athletic Club home games from Recreation Park in east Spokane to Natatorium Park, a public trolley park that also was home to top-notch city league baseball contests and a large swimming pool located at the west end of Boone Avenue along the Spokane River.

As Varnell was settling into his new role, club leaders tossed another curveball. On August 27, the board brought in Mike "Dad" Butler, one of Varnell's track coaches at the 1904 Olympics, as its athletic director, "… at a larger salary than any athletic director has ever received in any club or college west of the Mississippi River."[9] The promise of money had driven the decision. Butler, while visiting the West Coast to promote several running events earlier that year, had sold the Spokane Amateur Athletic Club board on the idea of hosting amateur boxing matches and wrestling tournaments—with Butler, of course, coming on staff to manage those potentially lucrative contests. Lester P. Edge, one of the club's directors, told the board, "Mr. Butler's duties will in no way conflict with the duties of physical director Varnell, but the two men will rather work in conjunction."[10]

Varnell continued his role with the mostly nonrevenue-generating sports, but also with a focus on football. By early September, he had found enough players—including three former college quarterbacks, an Army lieutenant, and a 285-pound local doctor who had designs on a starting fullback job—to field a team. A half-dozen of those players were slated to play in the backfield. Varnell was one of them.

The Spokane Amateur Athletic Club Rams held their first practice September 14, two weeks before the season opener against Spokane High School. The team's roster was ever-evolving and ever-improving. One day before the game, two ringers from Minneapolis joined the squad: J.T. Ludwig, a 214-pound former University of Minnesota quarterback/halfback; and Charles Murch, a 180-pound lineman. But those new players would have to wait a bit for their first game, because come game day, there was no open field in the city. Varnell and Spokane High's manager, George Rouse, agreed to move the game back a week to October 5, but the agreement was overruled by Rouse's boss, who already had scheduled a game for Spokane High that day against the University of Idaho.

The Rams continued to expand their already-beefy roster over the next two weeks, leading up to their (real) first game against the University of Idaho on October 19 in Moscow. Taking a page out of master recruiter A.A. Stagg's book, Varnell brought in more high-profile players from across the country and also increased the frequency of practices from three times a week to daily. In the week leading up to the game, the Rams added blue-chippers Joe Malcomson of Detroit, a former Chicago Athletic Association sprinter, boxer, and college quarterback; Wiley Lasater, a former Whitman College fullback and tackle; F.W. Woodland, a 214-pound center who had played the previous year for the Seattle Athletic Club; and Charles Reeve, a lineman on the previous year's Drake University team. At this point, and in an era when a 200-pound player was rare, the Rams' offensive and defensive linemen *averaged* more than 200 pounds per man.

Varnell did his best to whip his late-arriving men into shape. He held twice-daily scrimmages in the week prior to the Idaho game, and then selected his top fifteen players, including himself. They all hopped an early morning Northern Pacific train on Saturday, October 19, out of Spokane for the afternoon game in Moscow. The game was refereed by Varnell's former Olympic teammate, gold-medal-winning pole vaulter Charles Dvorak, who had moved to the area and soon would become Idaho's athletic director. The game was a defensive battle until near the end of the 25-minute-long first half, when Rams quarterback Sid Mulvihill fumbled a punt near his own goal line. Idaho—which had tied with Spokane High School, 0-0, two weeks prior—scored a few plays later. In the 20-minute-long second half, the Rams ran out of gas. Idaho scored three more touchdowns en route to a 22-0 win. Coach Varnell, who played the entire game at left halfback, attributed the defeat more to his own team's lack of conditioning than to any Idaho strengths. "[Varnell said] the defeat would help the team more than would have a victory as the boys have all expressed a readiness to get out regularly in the future that the team may not lose again through lack of condition,"[11] *The Chronicle* reported.

Varnell used his team's eagerness to train them harder the following week, but by the time that Saturday's game against Washington State College in Pullman approached, it appeared his plan had backfired. On Friday evening, as Varnell was finalizing his lineup, he received excuses from player after player that they would not be able to travel with the team. "Nothing except a hard beating seems in store for the club men,"[12] *The Chronicle* subsequently reported. *The Spokesman-Review*, which typically paid far less attention to the Rams than its rival paper, felt Varnell's squad would show better than it had the previous week.

The Chronicle's prediction came closest. Competing with four players who had never practiced with the team and with two others who had never played football, Varnell's Rams were thrashed by Johnny Bender's undefeated squad, 70-0. Varnell was his team's star on both offense and defense, playing "[a] great game at halfback and once [coming] near getting away with a clear field for a score."[13]

Varnell was able to keep most of his team intact, and bring back a few of the previous week's absentees for the next game, against the University of Montana. The team was late getting to Missoula, having to wait for former UW football star Homer Tilley to finish a late-night wrestling match so he could join the overnight train ride. The game was scoreless until early in the second half, when first-year Montana coach Albion Findlay, tired of his team's ineptitude, inserted himself at halfback. The former University of Wisconsin All-American then scored the game's only points and led Montana to a 12-0 win. Varnell again starred at halfback for the Rams.

The Rams had two weeks to prep for the opening of their league season, a series of four interclub games. Player interest surged. A week later, Varnell had thirty-three players on the field, including Tilley and city league baseball standouts Howard Slater and Dr. T.E. Callahan, who was reported to be a former professional pitcher. The roster even included the coaches of two of the teams to which the Rams already had lost: Montana's Findlay and Washington State's Bender. Controversy ensued. "This forms an 'amateur' athletic club," *The Chronicle* pointed out. "About a year ago, the Spokane Amateur Athletic Club made a stand for amateurism and withdrew its team from the city baseball league, warned its members that by playing with the city league they would disqualify themselves ... Suppose some college in the northwest would attempt to play Varnell, Findley [sic], Bender, Callahan, Slater and Neumann in its team. The probability is that the team might suddenly find itself without a schedule."[14] But, as the paper also pointed out, other athletic clubs in the Northwest also were using nonamateurs. The Seattle Athletic Club's roster, for example, included professional pitcher and former University of Washington athlete Dode Brinker of the Aberdeen Black Cats; former Michigan lineman and University of Washington head coach James Knight; current Washington coach and former Dartmouth star Victor Place; and former professional football player and then-pro wrestler Ben Roller, a barrel-chested Illinois doctor who commanded more than $1,000 for a single match.

Varnell spent the last week of preleague practice teaching his team from his Stagg-influenced playbook and running them into shape. On consecutive days, the Rams even held two no-contact scrimmages against Spokane High School.

When the Multnomah Athletic Club of Portland, Oregon, took to the field at Natatorium Park for a light scrimmage on gameday morning, it was clear Varnell's recruiting had paid off. The Port-landers looked much slower and smaller, a fact confirmed when the teams submitted their starting lineups to umpire Charles Dvorak. At 240 pounds, Callahan was by far the heaviest player on the field, and Spokane's eleven averaged 186 pounds to Multnomah's 183.

The game's first half—played in front of a small but enthusi-astic crowd of Spokanites—was scoreless and sloppy, with Mult-nomah's best drive ending with a missed place kick from Spokane's 25-yard line. Spokane's best shot at a score came on the ensuing possession, after Tilley gained 16 yards on a handoff off a fake pass, taking the Rams to Portland's 17-yard line. Varnell then lined up for a scoring kick that was blocked.

Spokane opened its playbook in the second half, and quarterback Slater began spreading the ball to Findlay, Tilley, and Varnell. Still, it was a fumbled punt by Portland that led to the only score of the game: a place kick from the 16-yard line by Dal Fotheringham. Multnomah missed a 16-yard kick of its own near the end of the second half that would have tied the game, and Spokane walked away with a 4-0 victory. Varnell caught several passes and smashed a 65-yard punt before exiting midway through the second half with a badly sprained ankle.

Spokane's win somehow caught the attention of the vaunted University of Michigan, which sent Varnell a letter offering to bring its team to town for a game later in the year. As Varnell discussed terms with Michigan's manager, he also continued recruiting players for his next league game, a 1907 Thanksgiving Day matchup at Natatorium Park against the Seattle Athletic Club. One week before the game, two more former college players joined the Rams, as did two players from Spokane's Blair Business College, and Charles Sigrist, a former standout tackle at the University of Washington.

Competitive chatter between the Seattle and Spokane clubs grew as game day approached. "We could beat the Spokane Amateur Athletic Club with our second team if we wanted to, but instead we are going to send our best team over to Spokane and wipe that bunch over there off the map,"[15] one Seattle manager told *The Chronicle*.

"Beat us with their second team?" Varnell scoffed. "Well they will have to go some. That bunch of bullies I have out every evening is showing up better every day and I would just like to see Seattle win that game with the best team they can muster from the whole Puget Sound country. If they do, I will take off my hat to them for it will mean that they have a fast, hard team."[16]

Coach Tom McDonald's cocky and bulky Seattle team arrived in town the day before the game, and held a practice that evening at Natatorium Park. On game day, Seattle pushed the Spokane team around the muddy field in the first half and scored twice in the second half to win, 10-0. Spokane's Findlay and Varnell starred, the prior making several key tackles, and the latter "… carrying the ball well and [once] pinning his man down with a thud on a tackle."[17]

Varnell suffered three broken ribs in the game, effectively ending his season. He gave his team a week off after the loss, before resuming practice on December 3. Two days later, his inability to play still eating away at his competitiveness, Varnell announced that he would be resigning at the end of the year. Spokane newspapers quickly picked up on the story, as did *The Seattle Daily Times*, which ran the following Varnell quote: "I resigned because of conditions ruling at the Spokane Amateur Athletic Club, but this is wholly because of the lack of interest by the members in the club teams. The people of Spokane are ready and willing to give support to clean amateur sport, but they will not stand for any other kind."[18]

Varnell had agreed to stick around until the end of the year for two reasons: First, that was when the job he had accepted across the river to help lead the athletic department at Gonzaga College—the Jesuit school where he had been moonlighting as head basketball coach—was to begin. And, second, he wanted to finish what he started and coach his team's final four games.

The Spokane Amateur Athletic Club's weekday football practices went on as scheduled, with Fotheringham taking over kicking duties in Varnell's absence and the roster continuing to rotate leading up to the team's last home game on December 14 against a Wallace (Idaho) Athletic Club team that earlier in the season had pushed the University of Idaho to its limits in a loss. On game day, however, the Rams dominated, winning 25-0.

On December 16, three Idaho players, including star quarterback Rodney Small, joined the Spokane team prior to its three-game, season-ending trip to the coast. The trek began with a Christmas Day rematch in Portland against Multnomah. This time, on a muddy, water-logged field, Multnomah exacted revenge and rolled to a 26-0 win. The next day, Varnell called for reinforcements: three

Washington State College players and the school's coach, Johnny Bender. As those new players were heading to Seattle for the New Year's Day contest against the Seattle Athletic Club, the Rams played a game against the Chemawa Indian School, a 600-student boarding school in Salem, Oregon, attended by youth from tribes across the western United States. Chemawa's sports teams competed at the highest level, with regular games against the universities of Oregon and Washington, as well as Stanford. Chemawa played physically against Spokane, one player hitting Fotheringham in the chest so hard that it knocked the Spokane fullback unconscious for more than an hour. Chemawa won, 11-5.

Spokane's final game against Seattle was, in essence, a Northwest club league championship. The Rams were 1-2 in league play, and a win against 2-1 Seattle would bring them even with that team and with 2-2 Multnomah for a three-way tie for the title. A Seattle win would mean an outright championship. Both teams were replete with ringers. Seattle's roster included University of Washington star Huber "Polly" Grimm; Henry Smither, a former all-American end from Yale who had just finished his first full season as head coach at Army; and two local high school coaches.

Spokane fullback George Hardy—one of the Washington State College stars—proved the difference, catching a short pass from his college coach and running 70 yards in the second half to score the game's only touchdown. Hardy also kicked the extra point to make it a 6-0 victory for the Rams.

Varnell, with his team, returned to Spokane by train the following day, his one-and-done season at the Spokane Amateur Athletic Club having concluded with three not-so-amateur wins, six losses, and a share of a league championship. The once-discussed game pitting the Spokane club team against the mighty University of Michigan never occurred.

GONZAGA

IMPLAUSIBLE THOUGH IT might seem today, given the school's status as a national basketball power, the first basketball game in Gonzaga College's new gymnasium was merely a postscript. There was no rowdy Kennel Club student section, no tournament banners hanging from the rafters, no first-round NBA draft picks.

The focus on February 21, 1905, was an evening-long celebration of President George Washington's birthday, and the official opening of the gym itself, a two-story brick-and-stone structure fronting Boone Avenue. In addition to a basketball court, the building featured separate rooms for reading, billiards, a debate class, and a museum. It was the final piece in the construction of Gonzaga's east wing, a section of campus built to accommodate the eighteen-year-old Jesuit school's growing enrollment, which that year alone had increased thirty percent to 353 students.

The basketball game took place halfway through the night,

following a gymnastics exhibition and a performance by the school band. It pitted the best players from the Gonzaga Athletic Club against members of the school's Junior Yard Association, which included an eighteen-year-old Montanan named Frank Walker, who would serve as U.S. postmaster general under presidents Franklin D. Roosevelt and Harry Truman.

Several students on the court had never played basketball prior to the practice sessions for this game, all of which were held in a snow-covered lean-to against the unfinished gym's outside wall. The game was won by the blue-and-white-clad Athletic Club, 15-6. The night's program closed with singing; drill-team performances by the Indian Club and military units; and tunes performed by an orchestra made up of sixteen boys, including Joe Albi, who would become an influential Spokane civic leader.

The gymnasium was a hit with the student body and community alike. *The Spokane Daily Chronicle* predicted the facility would allow basketball to overtake baseball as the school's most popular sport. Within a year, Gonzaga's unsanctioned teams were winning games against outside squads, including the junior-varsity teams of the Spokane Amateur Athletic Club, the Tiger Athletic Club, and local high schools. At the end of January 1906, for example, Gonzaga had a 6-1 record, having outscored its opponents 150-79. But basketball—unlike the comparatively well-funded baseball team, which had been around since the school opened in 1887—was not quite ready to claim its spot atop Gonzaga's sporting throne. For one, basketball still was unfunded and officially without a coach.

George Varnell's arrival in January 1908 as leader of Gonzaga's athletic department proved game-changing for the new sport. While still working for the Spokane Amateur Athletic Club, he had acted as volunteer coach of the school's basketball team and also officiated its games as his schedule allowed. As a paid coach, Varnell was stepping into a favorable position. Gonzaga's formidable starting five featured Rudolph "Bish" DeMers at center, forwards Johnny Healey and Tom Finnegan, and guards Bill Mulligan and Earl Healey.

Twenty-five-year-old George Varnell boards a train in
Chicago in 1907 en route to a new job in Washington. He
began coaching Gonzaga College's football and basketball
teams that same year. (Varnell family photo)

Varnell's coaching, and the day-to-day guidance from manager Joseph Van Hoomissen, produced a well-disciplined team
that tore through the 1907-08 season, finishing as champions of
Spokane's independent league with a 9-2 record, the only losses
coming against higher-division foes at Washington State and Whitman colleges. The latter was a 26-15 defeat in late January that
The Spokesman-Review felt Gonzaga lost only because its players were
outweighed by an average of 20 or more pounds per man.[1] In col-

George Varnell, far left, and his 1908 Gonzaga College football team.
(Gonzaga University, Foley Library Special Collections)

lecting its nine wins, Gonzaga twice beat the Spokane Armory Athletic Association, Blair Business College, and the Sprague Athletic Club. Gonzaga also defeated Pendleton (Oregon) High School, Cheney Normal School (now Eastern Washington University), and Bellingham Normal School (now Western Washington University).

Spokane newspapers never mentioned Varnell's name in conjunction with Gonzaga's basketball team, nor for any other coaching he did that year. Still, Varnell received his share of media coverage during that period, mostly as a result of his play on the baseball field. For several games during the winter of 1908, Varnell starred at shortstop for the Spokane Amateur Athletic Club's indoor team, his multiple-hit games and glove wizardry earning him the nickname "Yogi." It is unclear where the nickname originated; baseball's most famous "Yogi," Lawrence Peter Berra, was not born until two decades after Varnell's baseball-playing heyday. Regardless, the "Yogi" nickname followed Varnell for the rest of his life.

Soon, though, it looked as if the Spokane Amateur Athletic Club's 1908 baseball season would be forced to prematurely end.

The day after a game in which Varnell doubled home the winning runs in the top of the eleventh inning against Blair Business College, league president Eddie Rothrock suspended the team for the season for violating league rules. Varnell was the issue. It was Kentucky University all over again. Rothrock and Blair officials believed Varnell qualified as a professional and should not have been allowed to play amateur sports. A story in that evening's *Chronicle* absolved Varnell of trying to hide his status, instead placing blame on team captain George Baker: "Baker went to Varnell and asked him to play. Varnell explained to him exactly the position in which it would place the club team, and asked to be excused, but Baker was insistent and said he did not care, he would take the chance."[2] The league's board of directors banned Varnell from the league but reinstated the team on the condition that the Blair contest be replayed without him.

Varnell had to wait until spring to return to the baseball diamond. This time, he was back at shortstop for Slater & Slater, one of five semi-professional clubs in the Spokane City League whose weekend contests were held at Natatorium Park, where admission was twenty-five cents a head. Batting fourth most of the year, Varnell finished the season with a .284 average, second in the league in plate appearances, and tied for fifth in hits. His teammate and team manager, Howard Slater, led the league with a .369 average, and both men were named to the all-star team. He also played third base and was acting captain that spring for another of Slater's clubs, The Hill Bros. Walkovers.

Over the next decade, Varnell made several other baseball all-star teams, including as a pitcher-hitter for the 1916-17 Spokane Amateur Athletic Club indoor team, the Skadans. He finished the year with an 11-3 record on the mound and a .390 batting average.

MEANWHILE, ACROSS THE COUNTRY, inside a Lexington, Kentucky, courthouse in June 1908, Katherine Emmal Varnell filed for divorce from her estranged husband, and the divorce became final a few days later. She had found another man and followed him to Alabama. George Varnell, at this time twenty-six years old, was officially single.

THE FLEDGLING BASKETBALL PROGRAM Varnell had inherited at Gonzaga was like an empty canvas to an artist—full of hope, prospects, and potential. In contrast, the school's football program he also had taken over as a side gig in 1907 had been a soiled print, one that once had been loved and proudly displayed, then torn from the wall and tossed in an attic to ungracefully age.

The first official football game on Gonzaga's campus had been played on Thanksgiving Day 1892, Gonzaga's greenhorns squaring off against the far more experienced Spokane Amateur Athletic Club in front of some 500 people watching from the sidelines of the bleacher-less 120-yard field. Both teams had worn the rudimentary football gear of the era, including leather "helmets"—actually, headgear with no protective shell—that did little to ward off concussions. Gonzaga's coach, prominent physician and former Notre Dame player Henry Luhn, wore canvas painters overalls as he walked the sideline. The football was watermelon-shaped. The game ended in a 4-4 tie, a disappointing outcome to the Athletic Club, but one that sparked a fire in Gonzaga's student body, which shouted for more of what they had witnessed. The wish was granted.

Games against Spokane High School or Blair Business College—sometimes both—were played for the next several years, and Gonzaga's football program looked destined to continue its growth. But in 1899, local and national protests over football's violent and too-often deadly environment led school administrators to ban students from playing football on anything above an intramural level.

Gonzaga was but one of several U.S. colleges that curtailed football programs around this time. Yet over the next decade, football slowly regained favor nationally, and on Gonzaga's campus, thanks to a series of rule changes, including the installation of the

Coach George Varnell, far right, and his 1909 Gonzaga College football team, as seen
in an October 1909 edition of The Spokesman-Review. (The Spokesman-Review)

forward pass and elimination of the "wedge play," where players
would hold hands and together pummel any unfortunate opponent
in their way. In 1907, a Gonzaga-affiliated team played one intercollegiate game, an October 22 contest against Blair Business College that ended in a scoreless tie. But the following day's *Chronicle*
ran a lead story in its sports section saying that the team had not
been sanctioned by Gonzaga, and the school's ban on intercollegiate football still was in effect: "Gonzaga will not turn out a football team this year which will be allowed to compete in any other
than interclass games, nor was it the Gonzaga team which played
Blair Business College at Natatorium Park yesterday. The faculty at
Gonzaga has forbidden football at Gonzaga this season for match
games with outside teams, and while the boys will be allowed to
play, they must play under some other name than Gonzaga."[3]

At least one unofficial account of that 1907 season lists Varnell as Gonzaga's coach.[4] No official documentation can be found
to corroborate that assertion, but years later in an interview, Varnell
confirmed he was the school's coach that year: "I probably coached
the only college team that never played [an official] game all season.
The Jesuit moderator who was supposed to line up our schedule took
a dim view of football. ... Each week he somehow failed to book
a game for the following Saturday."[5] Varnell certainly *could* have
coached the 1907 game. It was played on a Tuesday, four days after
his Spokane Amateur Athletic Club team had played Idaho in Moscow and three days before it played Washington State in Pullman.

Thanks to a push from Gonzaga's athletic director, and former football star Father William Garrigan, school administrators fully reinstated football in 1908. Five local men, including Varnell, applied for the head coaching position. In the middle of August, the job was offered to Joe Morton, a Gonzaga and Georgetown University graduate and a former Georgetown football star then practicing law in Spokane. But some time over the course of the next three weeks, Morton either lost the job or declined the offer, and Varnell was hired instead.

Thirty-two men showed up on the practice field September 15, 1908, for the first school-sanctioned training of the Varnell regime. Enthusiasm throughout campus was high, but expectations for the "Fighting Irish"—Gonzaga's nickname bestowed by its first coach, former Notre Dame player Luhn—were low. Average player weight was less than 150 pounds, and experience was almost nonexistent. For three hours, Varnell led the wannabes through conditioning and basic drills, teaching them how to fall on a fumbled ball, field punts, and tackle. It was then that Varnell made his decision: Games this year against the larger regional colleges, such as Washington State and Idaho, would not be in his team's best interest.

That first week, Varnell chose 160-pound senior Tom Finnegan, star of Gonzaga's basketball and baseball teams, to be captain and one of his starting halfbacks. Junior Bill Mulligan, also a basketball star, was expected to start at the other halfback position. The next week, Varnell closed practices so he could install plays and hold daily scrimmages.

On Saturday, October 10, 1908, dressed in spotless blue jerseys with white-and-blue socks to match the school's colors, The Fighting Irish held their first official football game in nine years, on a makeshift on-campus field, yard lines freshly painted. The opponent was Spokane College, a year-old Lutheran-built school that was home to about 180 high-schoolers, bachelor's-degree candidates, and law school students. It was the second full season of football for the Spokane College Chieftains, but they did not appear to be the more experienced squad. Under the vigilant gaze of a sideline-pacing, bowtie-wearing Varnell, the Gonzaga team, which outweighed its opponent by an average of 10 pounds per man, held Spokane without a first down in both of the 20-minute halves on its way to a 50-0 win. Captain Finnegan scored several touchdowns, including one on a 105-yard kickoff return.

In an era when coaches' postgame comments rarely were recorded, Varnell had the advantage of voicing his opinions in print, thanks to his day job as a sportswriter at *The Spokane Daily Chronicle*. And in his nonbylined "Unappointed Referee" column the week following the game, he did just that: "The first game played by a Gonzaga football team in nine years was a great success from a Gonzaga standpoint. If the team can keep it up, Gonzaga will once more be placed on the football map."[6]

That Monday, three former University of Montana junior varsity players joined Varnell's squad as it prepped for its October 22 home game against Cheney Normal School. Cheney fans commissioned a train to carry 100 supporters to Spokane for the game, but the extra support did not help. In front of its own spirited booster squad, which clearly outnumbered that of the visitors, "Coach George Varnell's clever college team,"[7] as *The Spokane Press* reported, achieved its second-straight shutout, winning 17-0.

Varnell also continued football refereeing. On November 6, he worked his first major college football game, a Pacific Northwest Conference contest pitting Whitman against Idaho in which Whitman's Vincent Borleske, a Spokane native who later became his team's coach, kicked three field goals in an 11-0 victory. Borleske later became mayor of Walla Walla.

Two days later, the Gonzaga eleven crushed the Loyola Athletic Club, 44-0. Then, on November 21 at Recreation Park, Gonzaga ended its season with a 12-5 win over its chief rival, Blair Business College—itself fresh off a victory over the University of Idaho— with Mulligan and Finnegan scoring Gonzaga's two touchdowns. Gonzaga students rushed the field after the win, hoisting the players onto their shoulders and carrying them to a nearby field, where celebratory bonfires were set and songs sung. The win capped a perfect, albeit short, return season for Gonzaga football, which finished with a 4-0 record. Following the season, each varsity player was given a sweater with a 10-inch-high purple "G" sewed on the front.

Varnell received much of the commendation. After the Blair win, *The Spokesman-Review* ran with the sports-page-topping headline "Varnell Gonzaga Hero." The paper reported, "Out at Gonzaga college, after the bonfires have died down and the student body has in some measure recovered its ability to speak above a whisper it is evident that the team performing this feat has had coaching of a superior class, and credit is being given to George Varnell."[8]

THROUGHOUT THE FALL OF 1908, several of Gonzaga's football players were doing double-duty with the school's basketball team, and Varnell was doing double duty as well, coaching both squads. But, to be fair, he was doing so in an era when "coaching" was a relative term. Coaches' salaries, when there *were* salaries, were at best supplemental—especially at a small Jesuit college in the Pacific Northwest. In such situations, coaching duties took a back seat to whatever the coach's main money-making job might have been.

Varnell's bosses at *The Chronicle* allowed him to attend evening practices and weekend games, but did not allow him to be on campus during the day to handle administrative duties such as scheduling. For basketball, that duty fell to the team's manager, a senior from Butte, Montana, named Marcus Boarman, who had been an often-injured tackle on Varnell's football squad. Home games against the universities of Oregon and Washington were discussed but ultimately did not happen. In the end, Boarman drew up a twelve-game season for Gonzaga, kicking off with a December 11 home game against Cheney Normal School.

Official practice began shortly after Thanksgiving in Gonzaga's gym, which also served as the main practice facility for the Loyola Athletic Club's team. Scrimmages between the two were common.

Varnell's 1908-09 basketball team was not short on talent. With the exception of the two Healey brothers, most of the starters from the previous year's 9-2 team returned, including stocky junior guard Bill Mulligan, a four-sport star who had been playing on Gonzaga's interclass basketball teams since 1905; forward and team captain Tom Finnegan; and center Rudolph "Bish" DeMers. The other two starters included Fred Suren—who played as a guard, yet was as tall as DeMers, and Bill Cochrane—who was as short as Coach Varnell—at forward. Reserves included Frank McKevitt, Cyril Fairhurst*, and Maurice Meagher.

That first official basketball season in Gonzaga's history played out as follows:

Gonzaga 69, Cheney Normal School 6: The 1908-09 basketball campaign tipped off at three o'clock in the afternoon on Friday, December 11, in Gonzaga's new gym against Cheney Normal, a 600-student teaching college located 20 miles southwest of Spokane. Although Cheney Normal had been playing college basketball since the turn of the century, Gonzaga looked like the far more experienced team. DeMers scored 30 points and Finnegan 24. **Record: 1-0.**

Washington State College 23, Gonzaga 17: One of the Northwest's best teams, Coach Fred Bohler's Washington State College squad stepped onto the Gonzaga floor on the afternoon of December 18 and stepped off it two hours later with a 6-point win. "The play was fierce all the way, and the Pullman boys had their hands full to win out,"[9] *The Chronicle's* story, likely written by Varnell, reported the next day. Finnegan scored all but five of Gonzaga's points in a game that was refereed by Bohler (it was a regular occurrence at the time to have a coach help officiate his team's games) and Gonzaga graduate and former player Earl Healey. **Record: 1-1.**

---

* Fairhurst became a prominent Tacoma lumberman, and his granddaughter, Mary Fairhurst, was elected to the Washington State Supreme Court in 2002 and served as chief justice from 2016 until her retirement in 2019.

Gonzaga's first official basketball team in 1908-09 included, from left, Coach George Varnell, Rudolph "Bish" DeMers, Fred Suren, Maurice Meagher, Tom Finnegan, Bill Mulligan, Bill Cochrane, Frank McKevitt, and manager Marcus Boarman. (Gonzaga University, Foley Library Special Collections)

Gonzaga 19, Spokane Amateur Athletic Club 14: Gonzaga's first game after an extended holiday break took place New Year's Day at the Spokane Amateur Athletic Club as part of the club's "Ladies Day" celebration, which also featured a three-round boxing exhibition, a wrestling match, and three vocalists at halftime. Although the Spokane Amateur Athletic Club's hobbled top player, Howard Slater, "played the best game of his life,"[10] Gonzaga still walked away with a win. **Record: 2-1.**

Gonzaga 26, Sprague High School 8: Sprague High School came to the Gonzaga gym on January 7 and played a physical game against the older players, yet Finnegan, DeMers, and Mulligan "distinguished themselves"[11] as Gonzaga outclassed the high-schoolers for a victory. **Record: 3-1.**

Los Angeles Athletic Club 26, Gonzaga 23: In the midst of a several-game road trip across the western United States and into Hawaii, the Los Angeles Athletic Club stopped by the snow-covered Gonzaga campus on January 12 and grabbed a three-point victory from the hosts. "The game was fierce and hard all the way, and on several occasions, time was taken out by the

Gonzaga players after they had been slapped to the floor by their heavier opponents,"[12] *The Chronicle* reported. Finnegan and Cochrane each scored 9 points for Gonzaga. **Record: 3-2.**

Gonzaga 53, Coeur d'Alene High School 16: Behind 14 points from DeMers and 12 points from Finnegan, Gonzaga jumped out to a 33-7 halftime lead and played its reserves the rest of the way in a home win on January 25 over Coeur d'Alene High School. **Record: 4-2.**

Gonzaga 32, Spokane Amateur Athletic Club 16: Despite the addition of two former college players in the four weeks since it last played Gonzaga, the Spokane Amateur Athletic Club again lost to its inner-city rival on January 29. Gonzaga, playing without captain Finnegan, was led by DeMers's 12 points. "[T]he Gonzaga lads started off with a rush and wound up with a hurricane," *The Spokane Press* reported. "The game demonstrated the superiority of the collegians over the clubmen beyond all question."[13] **Record: 5-2.**

Gonzaga 40, Bellingham Normal School 8: Minus Mulligan, who had missed the entire week of school due to illness, Gonzaga beat Bellingham Normal on February 9 at Gonzaga, with DeMers and Cochrane scoring 10 points each. **Record: 6-2.**

Gonzaga 19, Whitman 12: With Mulligan rejoining DeMers, Finnegan, Cochrane, and Suren in the starting lineup, Gonzaga beat Whitman in Spokane on February 11. "The two teams scrapped from the first whistle to the last,"[14] *The Spokesman-Review* reported. "They banged each other against the wall and slammed each other around the floor, and at one time referee Johnny Bender had to rush in to prevent actual blows." The following day's *Chronicle* published the only team photo known to exist of the 1908-09 squad. Though the photo the paper used included Varnell at far left, the newspaper cropped the coach out of its printed product. **Record: 7-2.**

Gonzaga 49, Almira High School 14: One of the hottest prep basketball teams in the region, Almira High visited Gonzaga on February 15 and left with a 35-point loss. Several of Gonzaga's Tyros, the name for the school's junior varsity players, saw early action. **Record: 8-2.**

Gonzaga 36, Spokane Y.M.C.A. 34 (OT): With Mulligan out due to an elbow injury and Suren out for undisclosed reasons, Gonzaga struggled to a 36-34 overtime win on March 1 against the Y.M.C.A. in a game held on the Y.M.C.A.'s home court. The stocky, square-jawed Eddie Mulholland scored the winning bucket for Gonzaga. **Record: 9-2.**

Gonzaga 54, Spokane Y.M.C.A. 16: Two days later, on March 3, with Mulligan again out—this time due to a commitment to Gonzaga's baseball team—but Suren back in the lineup, Gonzaga dominated at home in a rematch against the Y.M.C.A. Suren and DeMers each scored 12 points for Gonzaga. **Record 10-2.**

Gonzaga won the Spokane city championship, but no celebration was held nor were any postseason games known to have been played, both due to the era and also because baseball season was underway, and a handful of other Gonzaga basketball players immediately left the team to join Mulligan to focus on that more-popular sport.

Despite Varnell's success as Gonzaga's basketball coach, both unofficially in 1907-08 and officially in 1908-09, he never again coached the sport. Perhaps more mysteriously, Varnell's name never could be found in any Spokane newspaper article about the Gonzaga basketball team during his coaching tenure.

When it came to his day job, however, the opposite soon was to be the case. In the newspaper industry, the name Varnell became pervasive and beloved.

DAILY CHRONICLES

THE **104,000 RESIDENTS** of Spokane, Washington, in 1909 had nearly a dozen sources feeding them news, including *The Orator-Outburst; Spokane Skandinav;* and *Industrial Worker,* a radical new weekly newspaper published to further The Industrial Workers of the World's mission of organizing and unifying the working class to help eradicate capitalism. For more frequent and mainstream reports, residents had one morning option, *The Spokesman-Review,* and two evening ones, *The Spokane Daily Chronicle* and *The Spokane Press.*

Operating under the motto "The Newspaper That Tells What It Knows Without Fear or Favor," the six-day-a-week, E.W. Scripps-owned *Spokane Press* was the underdog of Spokane's dailies, its history just seven years long. Its haphazardly designed eight pages of content were produced by a small team of locals, supplemented with reports from other regional Scripps papers and the Scripps-owned United Press Association, a 380-newspaper-strong news service. The public nicknamed the paper "The Penny Press," both because it cost just 1 cent and also because readers teased that it was not worth any more than that.

With histories dating back to the 1800s, the slightly left-leaning *Chronicle* and the right-leaning *The Spokesman-Review* were the city's real heavyweights, battling for advertisers, scoops, and subscribers, yet sharing a common goal of promoting their growing flagship city.

Oddly enough, both papers were owned by the same man, a Yale Law School graduate and former *Chicago Tribune* reporter named William Cowles. He had purchased *The Spokesman-Review* in 1894 and *The Chronicle* in 1897, the latter from one of Spokane's most prominent citizens, John J. Browne, but had allowed each staff to continue working independently. Thus, even under common ownership, the rivalry remained strong.

Both papers were printed seven days a week: *The Spokesman-Review* going out to 38,000 readers and *The Chronicle* to a few thousand fewer.[1] Page counts for each fluctuated between eight and thirty-two depending on the day, with sixteen pages the norm.

GEORGE VARNELL HAD ENTERED Spokane's newspaper battle in early 1908. Following in the footsteps of many ex-athletes of the day—including his former University of Chicago teammate Walter Eckersall, then working at the *Chicago Tribune*—Varnell had started as a sportswriter for *The Chronicle*, covering events he was playing in, coaching, or refereeing, as well as others to which he was assigned. Then, later in 1908, he was promoted to sports editor when Spokane-born and Stanford-educated Eddie Rothrock was promoted to lead the city desk.

Varnell, like Rothrock before him, had minimal assistance producing *The Chronicle's* sports coverage. Most days, he was the only staffer dedicated to athletics, his only help coming via reports to a phone that Varnell mainly manned. Cigarette in hand, he fielded reports on minor league baseball games; college and high school sports; and amateur events hosted at the Y.M.C.A., the Spokane Amateur Athletic Club, and other venues. He also wrote a regular column entitled "Unappointed Referee," a commentary roundup full of sometimes-critical, paragraph-long takes on happenings of note in the local, regional, and national sporting world.

The newspaper's policy of not allowing its writers to themselves *become* the news is the likely reason Varnell's name never appeared in its pages as a source, even when his Gonzaga basketball team was winning the city championship, and also why he had been cropped out of the team photo *The Chronicle* had published after a victory in February. Moreover, it is probable that it was Varnell himself who made many of those decisions. Additionally, Varnell even starred on the in-house editorial baseball team, which played weekly games against the newspaper's compositing team and teams from *The Spokesman-Review.*

When Varnell took over, *The Chronicle's* sports section typically consisted of a half-page tucked somewhere in the paper's front section, almost always topping a page anchored with ads for such items as luxury velvet ladies' hats; wool men's suits; and $5 outfits for young boys from the IXL Clothing Company, the purchase of which during one fall campaign earned the buyer a "dandy new football."[2] Often, a similarly structured additional half-page of late-breaking sports reports could be found further on in the paper.

One of Varnell's first accomplishments as sports editor was to consolidate those pages into one, typically ad-free page living underneath the header "Live, Up-To-Date News Of The Sporting World." Varnell made the most of his column inches, cramming a couple dozen national and local one-, two-, or three-paragraph stories about baseball, billiards, bowling, boxing, and football on the same page with team photographs, player sketches, and editorial cartoons. In an era when bylines were uncommon, *The Chronicle* readers first learned Varnell was the one curating, if not writing, all their sporting news in January 1910, when a box containing the words "Edited By George M. Varnell" first appeared atop each freshly redesigned sports page.

In October 1909, Coach George Varnell (number 1, at far left) brought a group of international runners to the Gonzaga College campus for a marathon race. Also included in the photo are Gonzaga athletic directors John Mootz (number 3) and Father William Garrigan (number 7), and eventual champion Henri St. Yves (number 8). (Gonzaga University, Foley Library Special Collections)

Varnell's civic activity continued during his tenure at the paper. In October 1909, he brought a team of internationally known marathon runners to Spokane, where they trained for two weeks on the Gonzaga campus and elsewhere prior to their November 7 race at Recreation Park. The race was won by a tiny French waiter, Henri St. Yves. Earlier that year, Varnell had staged a track meet in Gonzaga's gymnasium in which one of his former Gonzaga athletes, Earl Healey, ran a 30-yard-dash in three seconds flat, setting what would have been a world record if one had been recognized for such a distance.

However, Varnell's employment at *The Chronicle*—especially because he was the paper's only sports staffer—limited his ability to do as many other sports-related activities as he might have liked. He remained coach of Gonzaga's football team through the 1911 season—a one-win, three-loss, and one-tie campaign that included a 52-0 victory over Rosalia High School, a 58-0 loss to Washington State College, and a 6-6 tie with a Gonzaga alumni team featuring many of Varnell's former stars. Work, and his growing reputation as a collegiate referee, kept him from attending many of his team's games, including the school's biggest victory to that point in history, a 17-5 upset over the University of Montana on November 5, 1910, at Recreation Park. That win—spearheaded by quarterback Frank McKevitt and speedy running backs Eddie Mulholland, Ralph Sweeney, Jim Moriarty, and Billy Roche—inspired Gonzaga's alumni association to immediately launch a fundraising campaign to create an on-campus field specifically to be used by the team. At the time of the win, Varnell was at Denny Field in Seattle refereeing as his friend Gil Dobie's University of Washington football team beat Idaho, 29-0. Gonzaga's rudimentary sports ground did in fact get built and was first used by the team in 1913. Varnell's final record as Gonzaga's head football coach—not counting the lone 1907 game—was 10-4-1.

Varnell also had officiated the University of Washington's football game two weeks earlier at Denny Field against Whitman College, a game that involved a controversial call he made that left Whitman's coach screaming. He also refereed several other local games that year, including a Washington State College contest in Pullman, where he for a moment forgot his role on the field. When one player dropped the ball, Varnell yelled: "Fumble!"

Then he jumped on the ball.

As the players piled on top of him got up, Varnell realized his mistake. He also realized there was no entry in the rulebook to determine to which team the ball should go when a fumble was recovered by a referee. Varnell improvised, and handed the ball to the Washington State lineman who had been first to jump on him.[3]

Varnell also refereed a late-December de facto high school national championship game between Wenatchee High and Oak Park High of Chicago at Denny Field. The game easily was won by the boys from the Midwest coached by Robert Zuppke, who later would coach the University of Illinois to four national championships. The high school game was called early when apples handed out by Wenatchee boosters were thrown and fights broke out.

After the game, Oak Park's manager complained his squad had been robbed of its fair share of gate receipts, and the game's umpire, a man named Best, was criticized for asking for more pay

George Varnell, at far right, as noted on the photo itself, referees a Washington-California football game at Denny Field in Seattle on November 13, 1915. Varnell was good friends with Washington coach Gil Dobie off the field, but Varnell's ability to remain impartial on the field never was questioned. (University of Washington Special Collections, UW29127)

than those involved in the contest felt he should have received. "[Best] has sued the management for $100 in fees," reported *The Wenatchee Daily World*. "George Varnell, the referee, was willing to accept $50 for his pay and asked no more, while Best, an inferior official, demanded $100. The management can be put down in the 'sucker' class if it meets Best's demands."[4] Many Washington state coaches—including those in Aberdeen and Tacoma—claimed that their squads could have beaten the Chicago team, and therefore should have been the ones selected to play for the title. Varnell told *The World* that was not the case. "Some man came to me at the close of the game and asked how Aberdeen would have fared in a contest with Oak Park. I told him that Aberdeen would have been beaten much worse than Wenatchee. ... Chicago simply has the best undergraduate team I ever saw."[5]

As Varnell's college coaching career wound down, so did his baseball-playing one. In 1910, at age twenty-eight, he manned first base for the semi-pro Brown Cigar team, run by Jim Brown, the brother of Spokane Indians manager Bob Brown. In 1912, Varnell was the Indians's official scorer, and in the middle part of the same decade, he was the head statistician for the Spokane City League. Varnell's last season playing baseball was 1915, when he captained the Spokane Amateur Athletic Club's Skadans in the Indoor Baseball League. Then thirty-three, Varnell made the league's all-star team as a hitter (with a .390 average) and a pitcher with an 11-3 record, thirty-six strikeouts, and six walks.

The following year, Varnell's older brother Claude, who had owned a minor league baseball team in Fort Wayne, Indiana, as well as his gaming hall in West Virginia, died of pneumonia at age 42.

OUTSIDE THE SPORTING WORLD, Varnell in 1911 became engaged to Martha Elizabeth Winston. The twenty-three-year-old woman was living in her family's recently built home at 2024 West Pacific Avenue in Spokane with her widowed mother, Virginia, and five of her nine still-living siblings, including thirty-nine-year-old Alex, a well-known attorney mired in the defense of the city's embattled acting chief of police. That one of the Winston children had become a prominent attorney was not a surprise. The children's late father was former Washington State Attorney General Patrick Henry Winston Jr., a North Carolina-born distant descendant of Patrick "Give me liberty or give me death" Henry and a "splendid specimen of physical manhood, strong, handsome and commanding,"[6] whose "head was large and Napoleonic, brow high and broad, nose large and aquiline, eyes bright, clear, [and] sunny."[7]

Like Varnell, "Colonel" Patrick Henry Winston—his nickname given as a joke because he served in the Confederacy only during the last month of the Civil War and never entered into battle—also had been a newspaperman, owning, co-owning, and/or working at three newspapers: *The Albemarle Times* in Winsdor, North Carolina; *The Spokane Review*; and *Winston's Weekly*, a heavily editorialized, self-serving Spokane political journal for which he worked as editor from its first issue on August 22, 1903, until his death at age fifty-six on April 3, 1904.

As noteworthy as Patrick Henry Winston's legal and journalism careers were, his political accomplishments had been even more remarkable. When Washington became a state in 1889, President Benjamin Harrison had appointed Winston as the U.S. attorney for Eastern Washington, a position he held until Grover Cleveland removed him during his second stint as president. Running under the Populist Fusion ticket as a Silver Republican, Winston also had, at various points, been a Democrat and a Republican. He became state attorney general in 1897, and his physical and mental health suffered during his single term. Winston frequently was away from the state, at one point reportedly spending several months in a Maryland sanitarium.

Patrick Henry Winston's wife, Virginia, was an influential woman. Born in Pittsburgh in 1851, she was the daughter of a millionaire lawyer and had married Winston when she was eighteen, first moving to the Winston family's homestead in North Carolina. Virginia and Patrick Henry stayed on the farm for fourteen years, until Patrick Henry moved to Idaho to take the job of registrar of the land office in Lewiston, an appointment given him by President Chester Arthur as a second option because Virginia reportedly had vetoed Arthur's appointment of her husband as minister of Zurich, Switzerland. Virginia came to Idaho three years later, seven children in tow. Shortly thereafter, the family moved to Spokane.

Virginia Winston always entertained in her home but lived a much quieter life than her outspoken husband. Six months before her death in January 1934, the eighty-two-year-old widow granted her first newspaper interview, reflecting on her childhood, and lamenting how "girls of today" could not sew, cook, or read, and on their lack of desire to parent: "The great trouble with women today is they don't want to raise children! I feel I can speak of that, for I gave up my life for children. I reared ten."[8]

Martha Elizabeth Winston was one of those ten, born October 17, 1887, in Lewiston. Although her father had died when she was a teenager, Liz, as she was known, had a fortunate upbringing, thanks in part to her older brother's successful law career. Her engagement to George Varnell made for a banner headline in the June 14, 1911, *Chronicle*, and the story underneath identified the prospective bride as "… one of the popular maids of the younger society contingent,"[9] and noted that both she and Varnell were well known in the Spokane community. The wedding occurred four weeks later, on July 12, with 200 people gathering in the front parlor of the 3,500-square-foot Winston home. Howard Slater served as George's best man, and Liz's sister, Sally, was maid of honor. The bride's relatives from across the country came to bear witness.

Patrick Henry Winston Jr. was a newspaper owner and the Washington state attorney general who once had served as the U.S. attorney in Spokane under presidents Benjamin Harrison and Grover Cleveland. He died in 1904, seven years before his daughter, Martha Elizabeth, would marry George Varnell. (Varnell family archives)

The newlyweds' honeymoon began on the northern Oregon coast in Gearhart, and although plans had been made to travel farther south, into California, the trip was cut short when Liz became homesick for her mother. For the same reason, even though George had put money down on a house on Spokane's South Hill, the couple decided to move near the Winstons into the Renaissance-style, brick-built San Marco apartment building.

On November 3, 1916, the Varnells' only child, Virginia Elizabeth, called Ginna, was born at 2028 West Pacific in Browne's Addition in a home owned by Liz's mother, who still was living

George Varnell's daughter, Virginia Elizabeth, was born November 3, 1916, in this house at 2028 West Pacific Avenue in Spokane. (Varnell family photo)

next door at 2024. In fact, Mrs. Winston's home once had been *part* of the couple's house until a few years prior, when the Winstons decided to remove the back portion of their home, move it to the lot they owned directly to the east, and create a separate home. Doctor E.R. Northrup oversaw Virginia's birth, earning $35 for his time.

George was home for the delivery but left the following morning, hopping a train for Eugene, Oregon, to officiate the rivalry football game between the University of Oregon and the University of Washington. Varnell was friends with both coaches, Washington's Gil Dobie and Oregon's Hugo Bezdek, his former backfield mate at the University of Chicago. That game, played in front of 10,000 people at Kincaid Field, ended scoreless. "[W]hen referee Varnell's dear old whistle ended the battle," the *The Seattle Post-Intelligencer* reported the following day, "the Washington rooters crowded onto the field and carried every member of the team, the scrubs, and even staid old Coach Dobie from the field. It was a tie game but it was as big a victory as a Washington team has had in years."[10] Despite that moral victory against his heavily favored Pacific Coast Conference opponent—who went on to win the Rose Bowl— and possessing a 59-0-3 record in his nine years at UW, Dobie was fired at the end of the season. The reason: his perceived role in a players' strike. In a letter sent to *The Daily*, the UW's student-run newspaper, Varnell came to Dobie's defense: "I believe the University of Washington is losing one of the best and most thorough football coaches in the country. … I have never seen a Washington team that was not coached to play clean football, and to my mind the style of game a team plays is nothing more than the reflection of their coach and the style he teaches."[11]

Liz and George Varnell take a break from swimming at Loon Lake northwest of Spokane in 1915. (Varnell family photo)

Varnell returned to Spokane to work and see his daughter, but was back in Oregon officiating another game the following weekend. Thus began a pattern he would follow for most of the next decade: working at *The Chronicle* Monday through Friday, and on the weekends refereeing out-of-town games during football season and other sports closer to home the rest of the school year, and helping out with local baseball leagues, mostly as a statistician, the remainder of the time. Sunday mornings, he always was home to attend church with his family at the downtown All Saints Episcopal Cathedral.

Varnell's tenure with *The Chronicle* included several noteworthy moments, the most prominent of which had nothing to do with his role as sports editor but rather as witness to a terrifying incident related to the April 15, 1912, sinking of the *RMS Titanic*. Nine days after the ship's catastrophic collision with an iceberg in the North Atlantic Ocean had left roughly 1,500 people dead, Varnell was manning his sports desk on a Wednesday morning when a Russian immigrant living at an Idaho lumber camp and going by the name of Charles Aleck (his real name was later found to be Basil Alexiev) came into the office, demanding to see the editor. When city editor Eddie Rothrock showed up, Aleck pulled a .38 caliber revolver purchased two days earlier from behind his back, shot Rothrock in the chest, and then again in the arm after the editor had fallen to the floor. Aleck fled, while Varnell and several other staffers gave chase. The gunman was wrestled to the ground and restrained by three painters who had been working in the hallway.

The Spokane-born Rothrock died almost immediately, and Aleck was taken to jail, where he informed police that revenge had been his motive. Several of those at his lumber camp, Aleck said, had ridiculed him for his odd "unnatural practices"[12] and told him *The Chronicle* had run a story about him with a headline as large as the ones that had accompanied the breaking reports of the *Titanic* disaster. It turned out there had been no such story, a fact Aleck could not have confirmed because he could not read English. Rothrock's murder was the end result of a cruel prank staged by Aleck's co-workers.

As one might expect in a fast-growing city such as Spokane, Varnell was part of, or witness to, countless other, less tragic, work-related highlights over the next several years. He reported on the 1917 Washington State men's basketball team that finished with a 25-1 record—including a tough 32-28 road win over the Spokane Amateur Athletic Club—and which years later was retroactively named national champion. He dutifully covered Spokane Indians baseball each summer, watching as future major league stars such as pitcher Vean Gregg and outfielder Stan Coveleski honed their

George Varnell, right, signals a touchdown during the Big Game between California and Stanford in 1928. Varnell was one of the first officials on the West Coast to regularly wear a striped shirt. (Stanford University Special Collections and University Archives)

crafts. He then saw his city lose its baseball franchise due to poor attendance and play.

In 1920, Varnell was named an honorary member of the University of Washington chapter of Sigma Delta Chi, a national journalism fraternity, and helped Joe Albi found the Spokane Athletic Round Table, an organization of prominent sports-minded boosters. The organization, which carried on until the 1980s, provided high school and college scholarships, sponsored several high-profile events—including the 1944 PGA Championship at Manito Golf and Country Club—and donated millions to the construction of Memorial Stadium in 1950.

AS EXCITING AS VARNELL'S DAY JOB WAS, his officiating career was even more so. By the end of the first decade of the 1900s, Varnell had become the go-to football official in the West, praised by newspapers in Pullman, Seattle, Eugene, Corvallis, Berkeley, and Palo Alto in their advance stories for their teams' home games.

Though the papers' praise of Varnell, or any official, would today seem odd, at the time, top football referees were stars in their own right—often on equal grounds with top players. Thus

BIG GAME REFEREE TRAVELS 1100 MILES

To bring a referee from 1,100 miles away just to officiate in a single football game is a rare thing, but that is just what California is doing to insure expert handling of the Big Game Saturday. Realizing that no football critic with a broad enough knowledge of American football had been developed in San Francisco, California agreed to the appointment of George Varnell, sporting editor of the Spokane Chronicle, as the referee for the Big Game. Varnell was the head official in the Washington-Whitman contest last Saturday and left Sunday night for the scene of the struggle. He will also referee the game with California here on November 13.

George Varnell is a former star football player of the University of Chicago. Varnell was Stagg's crack halfback in the days of 1902 and 1903. While not a big man, he was one of the most feared men on the Maroon team because of his speed in circling the ends.

After leaving college Varnell took up newspaper work and for the last nine years has been sporting editor of the Spokane Chronicle. During that time he has been in charge of nearly every collegiate championship game in the northwest.

During Varnell's day, established football officials often were more popular than players, their accomplishments frequently earning newspaper headlines. This clip was written about the distance Varnell traveled to get to California to referee a Washington-California game. (University of Washington Daily)

historic stories from Varnell-officiated games are abundant and well-documented. One famous Varnell story took place in the fall of 1909, while he was in Salem, Oregon, working the Willamette-Oregon Agricultural College (later Oregon State University) game. On the game's first possession, Willamette's defense forced an Oregon punt, and the punter booted the ball over the end of the field, where it landed in a water-filled millrace, pointed downhill toward the mill wheel it powered. "[These were] the days when only one football was brought out for competition, and not a very good one at that," Varnell later said. Without a football, head referee Varnell had to make a call. "We decided to go after the one in the stream, and players, coaches, and fans joined in the race. We headed off the ball about half a mile down the millrace and finally got the game started again, putting the pigskin on the 20-yard line as if it had been downed behind the goal posts."[13]

Varnell's refereeing profile continued to rise during the 1910s. On any given Saturday, it was not uncommon for him to be more than 1,000 miles from home, the entire distance covered by train, at a cost in the hundreds of dollars to the host school. The miles Varnell traveled were themselves newsworthy. "To bring a referee from 1,100 miles away just to officiate in a single football game is a rare thing …," the University of Washington *Daily* wrote prior to a Washington-California game in November 1915, "[but] Realizing that no football critic with a broad enough knowledge of American football had been developed in San Francisco, California agreed to the appointment of George Varnell …."[14] That game—an early version of the "Big Game," which today is the annual rivalry between California and Stanford—ended with Washington winning, 72-0.* "George Varnell refereed a perfect game. He was on top of every play, and his penalties … were received without a protest," concluded the *Oakland Tribune*.[15]

Other noteworthy games Varnell officiated included Washington's October 31, 1914, contest against Oregon Agricultural College. The game, played in front of 2,500 fans on a muddy field in Albany, Oregon, ended in a scoreless tie, snapping Washington's 39-game winning streak. During the game, a controversial running-into-the-punter penalty on Washington's Mike Hunt got the UW star ejected from the game by Varnell, forcing Coach Dobie to use several first-time players to try to replace him. Washington's record heading into the 1914 Oregon Agricultural game was 4-0, its wins coming against Whitman College, Washington Park and Rainier Valley athletic clubs, and Aberdeen (Washington) High School, the latter a 33-6 home win on Denny Field.**

As in demand as Varnell was in the Pacific Northwest, it was in

---

* California and Washington played each other in the Big Game during the 1915, 1916, and 1917 seasons because California's traditional rival, Stanford, did not field an official football team during those years.

** In recent years, Varnell's descendants have worked with the University of Washington to recognize and preserve the Denny Field site, located in the northern section of the college's campus. The site is now a fully functional turf field frequently used by students.

George Varnell, far right with back to the camera, was head referee
for the muddy 1922 Rose Bowl game featuring California and
Washington & Jefferson. (Pasadena Tournament of Roses)

Southern California, in Pasadena, where he made his grandest officiating mark. Including the four years when the game was known as the Tournament East-West Football Game, Varnell worked eight Rose Bowls in that city, beginning with the World War I-affected 1919 game. At the time, the Rose Bowl was perhaps the most important college football game in the United States, and Varnell worked some of the most memorable of them all. A summary of those games in which Varnell officiated—early on as a head referee and later as an umpire or a linesman—follows.

January 1, 1919: Great Lakes 17, Mare Island 0. This was the second straight Rose Bowl to feature military squads, as college rosters across the country had been depleted by students serving overseas during World War I. Some 27,000 fans witnessed the game, won by a United States Navy team from Great Lakes, Illinois, over a Marine Corps team from Mare Island, California. The Navy squad was led by future NFL Hall of Fame coach and Chicago Bears owner George Halas, who had a 77-yard interception return and scored on a 32-yard pass reception.

January 1, 1920: Harvard 7, Oregon 6. Major college football's return to the Rose Bowl drew an additional 10,000 fans to Tournament Park's wooden bleachers than had the previous year's military-based game. The game's lone touchdown, by Harvard running back Freddie Church, and subsequent extra point, proved enough for the Crimson to defeat Oregon. Three weeks after the game, Varnell was featured in a film about the game and its accompanying parade. The film was shown in theaters across the country, including on the big screen of the Liberty Theatre in Spokane. The game was played the same year sportswriter Varnell came to know a Gonzaga University freshman by the name of Harry L. "Bing" Crosby, then a freshman member of the school's baseball team and also of its Junior Yard Association basketball team. Years later, after Crosby had become an international music and film star, Varnell took his family to California, where they connected with Crosby, who, as family legend tells it, was surprised Varnell still remembered him.

January 1, 1921: California 28, Ohio State 0. The presence of a team from California helped attendance rise to a record 42,000 in this Rose Bowl. The game itself proved a major mismatch, as the University of California crushed Ohio State University. This was one of several games Varnell officiated alongside his former teammate-turned-newspaperman, Walter Eckersall. In an interesting side note, 1921 was the first year referees began wearing zebra-striped shirts, meant to help better differentiate them from players. Varnell eventually became one of the first western officials to adopt that practice.

January 2, 1922: California 0, Washington & Jefferson 0. California's return to the season-ending contest was nowhere near as spectacular as it had been the previous year, as the undefeated and heavily favored Golden Bears of the Pacific Coast Conference could not get on the rainy field's scoreboard against Pennsylvania's tiny Washington & Jefferson College, and the game ended in a scoreless tie. Varnell was head referee for this contest, while Eckersall worked as field judge—and also covered the story for the *Los Angeles Times*. One page turn away from Eckersall's piece was a short article on the distances traveled by the four officials. In total, some 17,320 miles were covered by train, including 1,700 by Varnell.

January 1, 1923: University of Southern California 14, Penn State 3. Home-field advantage went to the University of Southern California in this one, as this game was the first played in the newly constructed Rose Bowl Stadium (previous games were played at Tournament Park), where USC had played three games earlier in the season. The Trojans fell behind 3-0 early, then scored touchdowns in both the second and third quarters to pull out a win over a Penn State squad coached by Varnell's former backfield mate at the University of Chicago, Hugo Bezdek.

January 1, 1924: Washington 14, Navy 14. Varnell's sixth Rose Bowl was the first for both the University of Washington and the Naval Academy, the latter which dominated the stat sheet but not the scoreboard, as the game ended in a 14-14 tie. One month after the game, *The Chronicle* ran a two-thirds page internal advertisement soliciting subscribers and touting Varnell's reporting. "Is there a human being in Spokane or the Inland Empire whose blood runs so cold that he is not interested in the red-blooded game of football? ... George M. Varnell, that fearless football referee, with a reputation as a football expert that is nation-wide, is sporting editor for *The Spokane Daily Chronicle*, and, with his knowledge of the game, combined with love and enthusiasm for this sport, paints a word picture so vivid and real that it is nearly equal to seeing the game itself."[16]

January 1, 1926: Alabama 20, Washington 19. Varnell's string of six consecutive Rose Bowls ended the previous year (Varnell missed the famed 1925 game in which Knute Rockne's Four Horsemen-led Notre Dame eleven defeated Glenn "Pop" Warner's Stanford squad, 27-10, but he did field and file a report on the game written by University of Washington head football coach Enoch Bagshaw), but he returned to Pasadena in 1926 as head linesman on Eckersall's officiating crew. The game—later remembered as the turning point for college football in the South—saw Washington's All-American running back George Wilson injured in the second quarter, and Washington subsequently lost a 12-0 halftime lead to eventually fall by one point to Alabama. Alabama scored all its points in the third quarter, when Wilson—who had been almost singlehandedly dominating the game—was on the bench. In front of 55,000 people, each team scored three touchdowns, but the Huskies made only one extra point, while the Crimson Tide made two. Varnell also wrote the front-page game story for *The Seattle Daily Times*. Today, the game often is cited as among the best college games in history. As an interesting side note, Alabama's star player was halfback Johnny Mack Brown, who won the Rose Bowl's MVP award and went on to become a film star, mostly in Westerns.

January 1, 1937: Pittsburgh 21, Washington 0. It took Washington returning to the Rose Bowl for Varnell to do so after an eleven-year hiatus. Varnell again served as head linesman, and the Huskies again lost, this time to Pittsburgh in front of a crowd of more than 87,000.

Varnell retired from officiating in 1946 with an impressive tally. He had refereed nearly 1,000 high school, college, and club contests.

VARNELL'S SPORTING REPUTATION vaulted him to celebrity status in Spokane and, in football circles, across a large portion of the United States. In fall 1922, *Sunset* magazine even sent a writer to Spokane to do a piece on Varnell. The article, titled "Interesting Westerners," featured a nearly half-page portrait of the referee, calling him "The Dean of Western Football":

> When sixty thousand excited partisan football fans lean forward in their seats in the huge stadium at the Stanford-California gridiron classic and see a short, stocky, white figure on the field make a decision upon which rests the outcome of the annual "big game," that decision is momentous … That short stocky figure needs no introduction … This man makes a decision every thirty seconds to a minute. He has never had one reversed. He isn't that kind of official. … His name is George M. Varnell, the "Walter Camp of the West."[17]

The story continued its praise for the entirety of its 600 words, concluding, "Football critics, fans and fellow officials generally consider Varnell to be the best official the West has produced."[18]

Though the event was not mentioned in the *Sunset* article, Varnell had been selected to swing the first pick into the gravel-laden soil on the Gonzaga campus in May that year in Spokane, breaking ground on a $100,000 multiuse wooden stadium project that was to include locker rooms, concession stands, restrooms, and a press box featuring state-of-the-art telegraph, telephone, and radio equipment. Gonzaga Stadium was completed five months later, and the home team hosted its first football game there on October 14, a 10-7 loss to Washington State. Gonzaga's season ended on Christmas Day with a 21-13 loss to West Virginia during the East-West Classic in San Diego, the only postseason appearance in school history.

In 1924, Varnell was elected to the influential National Football Rules Committee, serving alongside the legend to whom *Sunset* had compared him, former Yale player, coach, sportswriter, and "Father of American Football" Walter Camp, his former coach A.A. Stagg, and several other dignitaries. Varnell served on the committee—which held annual meetings in New Jersey or New York—from 1924-29, a period when several important changes were made to the college game, the rules of which were at the time mimicked by the professionals. Changes implemented or adjustments made during Varnell's tenure included: The repositioning of goal posts from the front to the back of the end zone; the requirement for any in-motion players to remain set at the line of scrimmage for at least one second before the ball was snapped; the introduction of a 30-second play clock and a 15-second limit in the huddle; and the implementation of a 25-yard penalty for a clipping violation.

"Clipping," Varnell wrote in 1925, "that particularly dangerous method of defense sometimes tried in a football game, will be a more serious offense this year. ... Probably more football players have received painful injuries as a result of clipping than any other [penalty] in football."[19] He also was the leader of a failed push in 1926 to eliminate the kicking option for the point-after attempt following a touchdown. "The try is an individual, not a team play, that it does not in itself necessarily represent team strength and therefore should be dropped from football," Varnell wrote.[20]

Varnell's Rules Committee work was an important part of the shaping of the game of football played today. Along with improved transportation and larger stadiums— which allowed more fans to attend games—and the forward pass, which opened the game and made it more exciting to watch, the contributions of Varnell and his com-

This portrait accompanied the 1922 Sunset magazine article on George Varnell that labeled him the "Walter Camp of the West." (Sunset)

mittee colleagues were instrumental to the post-World War I transformation of college football into the higher-scoring, offense-friendly game we know today.

UNTIL THE FIRST WORLD WAR, many newspapers—and later, radio stations—had provided in-depth reports of teams only in their own coverage areas. Yet in the 1920s, as the game's popularity grew, local media also began to offer detailed reports on nonlocal teams as well. Readers from Spokane to St. Petersburg, Florida, were treated to Sunday pages filled with large photographs from the previous day's games and romanticized words from national writers such as Grantland Rice, whose football-related nicknames for players such as "The Four Horsemen" and "The Galloping Ghost" became household terms. College football had become big business, and the media played a major role.

Varnell's reputation within that football circle brought him many unsolicited employment offers, including from the Pacific Northwest's two biggest cities. In early December 1924, he received a job offer from the Multnomah Athletic Club in Portland, Oregon. The club—for years a key rival of Varnell's former employer, the Spokane Amateur Athletic Club—wanted Varnell as its manager. On the third page of its December 6 edition, *The Bulletin* of Bend, Oregon, reported an update on the offer: "[Varnell is] one of the foremost officials on the coast. [But he] has not yet made known his decision."[21]

His decision was "no," partly because of a more appealing offer he had received earlier that month. In mid-December, Varnell accepted that other offer: to become a sportswriter for *The Seattle Daily Times*.

When announced, Varnell's decision to leave Spokane made headlines in several newspapers, including *The Chronicle*, which informed its readers via a page-one, above-the-fold story on December 29. Varnell's co-workers, family, and friends had known about his pending move for a couple weeks, and several going-away parties already had been thrown, the largest one held downtown on December 26, 1924, at the Dessert Hotel. The event was hosted by The Knights of the Round Table, and the pun-filled, football-themed menu included a "kickoff cocktail," "soup a la whistle," "tackle steak," "scrimmage potatoes," "onside salad," and "rolls, out o' bounds." A sheet of paper accompanying the menu on each silk-tablecloth-draped table included a large photo of a bespectacled, mustachioed Varnell, and a dedication to the honoree written by The Knights: "Here's hoping, old Top—that the new kickoff finds you ready to return the ball for an all the way touchdown."

Three days later, following a gathering of co-workers, friends, and family at the majestic Davenport Hotel, Varnell left the city aboard a Spokane, Portland & Seattle Railway car to Portland, then hopped another train to Berkeley, California, to referee a New Year's Day postseason football game between California and Pennsylvania (his commitment to that game caused him to miss working that year's Rose Bowl game between Notre Dame and Stanford). Varnell's last bylined piece in *The Chronicle* ran atop the sports section on December 31, 1924. It was a story about his selections for the first- and second-team all-Pacific Coast Conference football squads. It was The Unappointed Referee's last judgment call.

GOOD *TIMES* IN SEATTLE

T ALWAYS HAD BEEN her most wonderful time of the year, but the holiday season of 1924 left Liz Varnell mirthless. The pending, and permanent, move west, across the mountains from Spokane to the much larger Seattle, had rinsed the usual gaiety out of the thirty-seven-year-old wife and mother of one, leaving a sense of dread no amount of large-family-fueled holiday cheer could counter.

For years, Liz had used her veto power to postpone this inevitable day, as job offers from Portland, San Francisco, and Seattle had come her husband's way. Given how often George Varnell had to work away from home, she was reluctant to leave the support of her family and friends. But when this latest opportunity came knocking, she knew it was one she should not deny her accomplished and ambitious mate. She *knew* this, sure, but that did not make the decision any easier. "When we moved to Seattle in 1925,

I think I cried every day I was over there," Liz said decades later. "I came home for a visit eleven times that year."[1]

She first had to leave Spokane, of course, and it took her a while to manage that. While Varnell was in Berkeley refereeing the California-Penn New Year's Day game, Liz Varnell and eight-year-old Ginna spent one last extended holiday season in Spokane. As the holidays faded, workers returned to their jobs, students to their schools, and the calendar flipped to 1925. But still mother and daughter remained east of the Cascades.

During the first week of January, four going-away celebrations were held in Liz and Ginna's honor. The second week, five consecutive days of parties were thrown, each one earning a small-headlined story in *The Spokane Daily Chronicle's* social pages. On the Tuesday of their departure, Liz and Ginna were feted at a luncheon at a friend's home on South Hill. Wednesday, they were the honored guests at a tea party in the home of close family friends. Thursday, Liz's mother and her sister-in-law hosted a tea party at the family home in Browne's Addition. Friday, a dinner was held in Liz's honor at the home of the Dessert family, owners of the hotel where two weeks earlier Varnell himself had been so grandly honored. And on Saturday, January 10, the day of Liz and Ginna's departure, another luncheon was held at another friend's home.

By the time his wife and his daughter arrived in Seattle, George Varnell already had settled into an apartment on Capitol Hill and had worked a full week at *The Seattle Daily Times*. Opportunity and one man's persistence had brought him there.

AS FOR THE OPPORTUNITY, the port city of Seattle was three times the size of Spokane and trending in the opposite direction. In the seventeen years Varnell had spent in Spokane, he had seen it transform from a post-Great Fire, railroad-fueled boomtown to a stagnant city with dwindling opportunities and stalled population growth. Seattle—largely thanks to its port and access to natural resources—still was booming, having grown nearly 200 percent in the 1910s to more than 330,000 residents.

With the folding of the Seattle Metropolitans hockey team in 1924—just seven years after it won the Stanley Cup—the quality of professional sports in both cities essentially was the same, with Spokane and Seattle hosting high-level minor league baseball teams. But with its college sports—Varnell's passion—Seattle was hands down the superior city of the two. The University of Washington offered several nationally competitive intercollegiate

Liz and Ginna Varnell in Spokane in October 1924, three months before their big move to Seattle. (Varnell family photo)

sports, including football, baseball, tennis, and track and field. That is not to mention the university's most celebrated program: its men's rowing team.

The sport of rowing had been prominent throughout the region more than three decades prior to Varnell's arrival. The Seattle Athletic Club, Varnell's one-time nemesis, had been racing in regattas since acquiring its first shell in 1893, and interest in starting the sport at the University of Washington followed when, in 1895, the school moved its campus north from downtown to a site between Lake Union and Lake Washington. The UW crew rowed its first official race on May 3, 1903, in Victoria, British Columbia, against the junior team from the James Bay Boat Club. Coached by UW football coach and former Princeton oarsman James Knight, the UW's four-person crew featured Knight's most muscular football players. They won by a quarter of a boat length. A month later, some 5,000 people lined the shores of Lake Washington to watch the same four oarsmen defeat the University of California in the first interstate collegiate regatta ever held on the West Coast.

In revolutionary cedar shells painstakingly crafted by Englishman George Yeoman Pocock, the UW team became a powerhouse, winning national championships in 1923, 1924, and 1926. UW coaches were something special, too. There was Hiram Conibear, considered the founding father of Washington Rowing, who, as a former professional athletic trainer and cyclist, had been the trainer of the University of Chicago football team the year Varnell played there. Conibear was followed by protégés Ed Leader and Rusty Callow, who continued his style of rowing at Washington. In Seattle, George Varnell had found himself a new sport to own and a university stroking its way to international renown on the oars of one of the greatest crews in rowing history—the legendary blue-collar "boys in the boat."

The persistent person who finally, after multiple attempts, was able to draw Varnell out of his stable Spokane shell was *Seattle Daily Times* publisher Clarence Brettun "C.B." Blethen, whose family had owned and operated the conservative-leaning newspaper since 1896. C.B. Blethen had a personal interest in the success of the Husky crew program: His son, Frank, had been named coxswain of the 1925 junior varsity team. So C.B. went searching for a writer he felt could adequately narrate the enthusiasm he felt for rowing. A writer he already knew well, Varnell, proved to be that man. Covering Husky crew and the college's other sports became Varnell's main duty.*

Sports coverage played a major role in the circulation battle between *The Times*, an afternoon paper, and William Randolph Hearst's morning daily, the *Seattle Post-Intelligencer*, aka "The *P-I*." When Hearst acquired the *Post-Intelligencer* in 1921, it became the

---

* The recent adoption of the "Huskies" nickname added luster to UW athletics. The university's athletic teams had been called the "Sun Dodgers" for several years, "but a lot of people thought that didn't do much for the school's—or the region's—image," UW historians note. "An attempt to adopt the nickname 'Vikings' in 1921 was met with protest by the students, and a joint committee of students, coaches, faculty, alumni, and businessmen proposed new names. The Huskies nickname for athletic teams was officially adopted on Feb. 3, 1922."

*The University of Washington's soon-to-be-legendary "boys in the boat"
crew, pictured here in 1936 outside the ASUW Shell House. (MOHAI)*

eighth link in a national chain that boasted 15 million readers. *The
P-I* immediately acquired access to Hearst's International News
Service and King Features syndicate, which provided commentary
by influential columnists, as well as color comics and *The American Weekly* Sunday supplement. "*The P-I* pulled out all the stops on
circulation promotions," John C. Hughes wrote in *Pressing On*, his
2015 book on the history of *The Seattle Times*. "The daily newspaper
was a smorgasbord of world and local news, politics, sports, and
entertainment," he wrote. Moreover:

> There were chic, full-page department store ads and page
> upon page of classifieds. Dad consumed the editorial page and
> sports section; Mom turned first to Society, then the grocery
> ads; Junior got Krazy Kat and Buck Rogers, and Sis the cin-
> ema section. Sports were big everywhere but huge in Seattle.
> ... The dueling Sunday newspapers hit the porch with an im-

pressive plop and, at 10 cents apiece, offered a moveable feast. C.B. Blethen countered the *P-I's* fat package of features with an 86-page Sunday edition of his own, including a classy Rotogravure pictorial section and eight pages of color comics.[2]

Varnell's stories and predictions—replete with the colorful sportswriter lingo of the era: the "scampering," "steamrolling," and "swivel-hipping"—would in due course become a key attraction for *The Times* in the fight of its life with its rival, *The P-I*. *The P-I* boasted that it sold 6,000 more copies daily than its afternoon rival and enjoyed a whopping 40,000-copy lead on Sundays.[3]

One of Varnell's first *Times* stories carried a byline that listed him as the referee of the 1925 New Year's Day California-Penn game. Two days later, on January 4, 1925, he officially was introduced to *Times* readers via a large, tightly cropped portrait and a seven-paragraph story on the third page of the sports section. The peculiarly themed piece centered on Varnell's success as a football official, made no mention of any previous journalism experience, and incorrectly listed him as a University of Chicago graduate. The story's lone quote was from UW's former record-setting sprinter, Vic Hurley, on Varnell's proficiency as a race starter in track.[4] Less clumsily, Varnell's name appeared in the masthead of the following day's sports section, listing him as an associate sports editor with a focus on football and other college sports. He shared the department's second-in-command duties with golf expert John Dreher, who a decade later would achieve front-page fame for his role in the return of nine-year-old George Weyerhaeuser to his family in Tacoma. The boy had been held hostage by kidnappers for eight days.

Dreher and Varnell, along with their editor, Cliff Harrison, worked hard to fill *The Times'* four-page sports section in the readership battle with both *The P-I* and the Scripps-owned *Seattle Star*, a daily with a blue-collar following. Varnell's observations were often tacked on the end of a commentary on current events written in a roundup fashion, not unlike his "Unappointed Referee" column

*An always well-dressed George Varnell in the newsroom
of* The Seattle Daily Times *in 1931. (Varnell family photo)*

during his earliest days at *The Spokane Daily Chronicle*. *The Times'*
version, called "Sportitorials," was penned on a rotating basis by
Dreher, Varnell, and Harrison, and bylined only with each writer's
initials. Curiously, the first time Varnell's surname—aside from its
daily spot in the masthead—appeared in the sports section was in
the middle of January 1925, in a story listing him as one of the competitors in an amateur doubles handball tournament.[5]

That winter, Varnell focused on amateur athletics, concentrat-
ing on local college basketball and local and national college football, and a joint effort by several Northwest cities to lure Olympic
champion distance runner Paavo Nurmi of Finland to Puget Sound
that spring to compete in a series of exhibition races.

University sports coverage was Varnell's primary focus and
love. He was on the UW campus daily, splitting time between former Olympian Clarence "Hec" Edmundson's track team, Dorsett
"Tubby" Graves's baseball team, and megaphone-toting Russell
"Rusty" Callow's rowing squad. Callow often took Varnell out
on the water with him as he coached his team, so the reporter
could learn rowing's nuances and terminology. Oftentimes, Varnell's reports would be a roundup of the day's happenings from all
three teams, including detailed notes from practices and ongoing,

in-depth season previews, including this one of the crew team from March 1925:

> One plus one is two. That's easy enough. The Washington stroke plus a gang of young giants makes a varsity crew. Just as easy. Washington has the stroke, there is no doubt about that fact for universities throughout the country have been adopting it, working on it, and trying to imitate it by using Washington graduates as coaches. Washington also has the type of oarsmen necessary to fit the stroke. The long, rangy athletes are in demand for the stroke and there are plenty of them on hand every afternoon at the varsity boathouse for Coach "Rusty" Callow to look over.[6]

Rowing was the only sport Varnell covered that he had not competed in himself, but crew still received a majority of his attention. His near-daily stories kept readers apprised of almost every move the popular oarsmen made and helped draw large crowds to Montlake to see each race—100,000 people would attend. Varnell even worked as a de facto fundraiser for the team, penning several pieces that year to help the team raise the $17,000 it needed for the trip to New York to defend Washington's back-to-back titles at the Poughkeepsie Regatta, the Intercollegiate Rowing Association's national championship. The fundraising was successful, and on June 6, 1925, Varnell was the only writer accompanying the UW rowers as they boarded the Northern Pacific Railway's 9:30 a.m. New York-bound *North Coast Limited* train. More than 1,000 people packed the landmark King Street Station for the Huskies' sendoff.

Varnell wired daily reports to Seattle, including one on June 7 from Chicago during a practice stopover, where, "The Huskies were treated like real celebrities [and] escorted to waiting automobiles where an escort of motorcycle police waited to lead the way through the crowded Chicago streets...."[7] Varnell's final report came June 23: a front-page take on UW's half-boat-length defeat to Navy. Frank Blethen, the son of Varnell's boss, had been in the JV boat that day.

*George Varnell and his daughter, Ginna,
in Spokane. (Varnell family photo)*

AS THEY HAD SOME TWO DECADES earlier in Spokane, George and Liz Varnell quickly became involved in the local scene, appearing in *The Times's* social pages for their attendance at one event or another. George appeared in stories about his former football prowess and also for his community service, in particular his hosting of occasional sports-related lectures.

George, Liz, and Ginna lived in an apartment at 1005 East Roy Street. Designed by renowned architect Frederick Anhalt, the apartment was the first in Seattle to feature an underground parking garage. Its French Norman and English Tudor design perfectly matched its across-the-street neighbor, the Tudor-style Lowell School, where Ginna attended seventh and eighth grades.

Ginna was a gifted student who had skipped sections of elementary school, and thus was the youngest in her class both at Lowell and at Broadway High School, from which she graduated in 1933. The Roy Street apartment, today a Seattle historical landmark, would remain Varnell's home for the rest of his life.

George Varnell, cigarette in hand, on the docks at Montlake, standing on the same slats as did "the boys in the boat" (see photo on page 133). (University of Washington)

NEARING THE END OF 1927, Cliff Harrison left *The Times* to work at *The Star,* and Varnell was named the paper's sports editor. Almost simultaneously, across town, 24-year-old Al Ulbrickson, himself less than two years removed from his stroke seat on several Husky championship shells, was selected to replace Callow as the University of Washington's head rowing coach. The University of Pennsylvania had wooed Callow with a large salary—some $12,000 per year—to lead its program. On his way out the door, Callow had endorsed Ulbrickson, the freshmen coach the previous year.

The program Ulbrickson inherited had lost a handful of seniors but had achieved national prominence and was expected by most to stay there. It also was the year Frank Blethen became the team's varsity coxswain. As sports editor, Varnell kept his UW Crew beat, and helped create and popularize a term that became vernacular in the sport for decades. At the time, the UW rowers were utilizing a shorter stroke than the lengthier, Oxford-style one most top teams employed. The UW stroke, a modified version of the efficient row used by the watermen who for centuries had ferried freight and passengers on the River Thames in London, had been brought to Seattle by master boat-builder George Pocock, who himself had raced shells on the Thames. When Pocock and his brother, Dick, eventually came to the UW to build shells for the team in 1913, George Pocock helped Hiram Conibear introduce the new rowing technique. Intrigued, Conibear studied the physics of the move, going as far as borrowing a skeleton from the biology department and equipping its hands with broomsticks to analyze the movements.*

Varnell created a contest for *Times* readers, asking for help naming the UW's distinctive stroke. "Conibear stroke" overwhelmingly won, and the stroke soon became commonplace at top college programs across the country, frequently after UW alumni went on to lead those programs. In fact, the stroke became so ubiquitous in the United States that many began calling it the "American" stroke.

Varnell's sports section faced tough competition from the *Post-Intelligencer.* Leading the charge for Hearst was the folksy Royal Brougham. The 33-year-old sportswriter had dropped out of high school in 1910 to work as an office boy at *The P-I*, running copy for sports editor Portus Baxter. Brougham rose quickly, becoming sports editor in 1923. With a great byline name and informal writing style, Brougham became a marquee attraction for the *Post-Intelligencer.* He punctuated his stories with personal anecdotes gleaned from his close relationships with his subjects. Slightly built, gap-toothed, slick-haired, and larger than life, Brougham was a popular personality in Seattle and beyond. Jack Dempsey, Babe Didrikson Zaharias, and Babe Ruth were among Brougham's many celebrity friends.

When Varnell came to Seattle in 1925, Brougham recently had been promoted from sports editor to managing editor. But in 1928, the year after Varnell became sports editor at *The Times*, Brougham was sent back to head the sports desk. His Christian

---

* Conibear died at the age of 46 in 1917, when he fell from a tree in his backyard.

faith had steered him away from publishing stories about Hollywood actress Marion Davies, who was having a well-known affair with William Randolph Hearst, whose parties at a hilltop retreat in California were the stuff of legends. Hearst required his editors to burnish his lover's movie career.

Back on the sports beat, Brougham's tell-it-like-he-sees-it reporting and observation-focused columns resumed their influential status in Seattle and beyond. He wrote a regular first-person column for *The P.I.* entitled "The Morning After," in which he referred to himself as "your old neighbor." "[He was] part poet and part P.T. Barnum, a promoter and self-promoter,"[8] one journalist wrote of Brougham years later. Yet much of Brougham's promoting was done to help individual Seattle-area causes about which he felt passionate. Brougham frequently emceed events, sports and nonsports, his persona outgoing.

Varnell and Brougham were rivals on paper but also friends who, particularly so in later years, reported on each other's accomplishments. But that did not stop readers from continuously picking favorites during each writer's heyday. "Did you compare the columns of Varnell and Brougham?" one UW alum once wrote to *The Times*, days after a heartbreaking 7-6 Husky football loss to Oregon State. "Varnell gave the Huskies plenty of credit and constructive criticism, but I oughta sock Brougham in the eye. Nuts to him, comparing the best team in the Conference with Blaine and Ferndale, Westwood and Colorado Military, and saying the Huskies are no good, so let's forget about it."[9]

The routine Varnell had adopted in Spokane, that of reporting during the week and officiating on the weekends, continued in Seattle, his refereeing endeavors in the bigger city almost completely dedicated to major college football. On November 26, 1927, for example, he worked a USC–Notre Dame game in front of an estimated 120,000 people—one of the largest crowds in history—at Soldier Field in Chicago, a 7-6 victory for Knute Rockne's Fighting Irish. Varnell also wrote a story about the game for his paper, a practice that today would be deemed a conflict of interest. At the

Liz and George Varnell. (Varnell family photo)

time, however, it was a cost-saving measure and not frowned upon. Varnell officiated crew races, too, most involving the same UW team he had been brought to Seattle to cover.

Like Brougham, the more-reserved Varnell wielded a large influence on Seattle's social scene. The first large-scale example came in 1928, when real estate speculator Noel Clarke moved to Seattle from Los Angeles and began lobbying to create an upscale, amenity-filled athletic club in downtown Seattle he wanted to call the Washington Athletic Club. Varnell, a former athletic club director, player, and coach, was the first to pen a piece in favor of the "WAC." A year later, Clarke's real estate license was revoked due to shady business practices, and he resigned from the club project. Varnell threw his weight behind the man who purchased control of the idea, William Comer. At the time, Varnell was an elected official of the Pacific Northwest Athletic Association, the governing body of the region's athletic clubs. The association admitted the Washington Athletic Club into its ranks in October 1929, giving the club's leaders the cachet they needed to proceed. Construction on the high-class club at Sixth and Union in downtown Seattle began a short time later. The $2.5 million, twenty-one-story building housing the club opened in December 1930, with storefronts at street level and the athletic club occupying the rest. The club included an indoor swimming pool; locker rooms; a dining room; pool, game, and card rooms; a bowling alley; a gymnasium; several sports courts; massage tables; steam baths; and a separate elevator for women.[10] Due to The Great Depression, the club was the last major building built in Seattle for several years. Varnell was one of the club's earliest members. Subsequently, the club itself nearly fell victim to economic downturns, but a variety of strategies—including the introduction of slot machines and liquor—helped it survive. The WAC since has been expanded and renovated several times, and survives as a Seattle landmark.[11]

Triggered by the 1929 Wall Street crash that affected much of the world and caused the largest economic contraction in history, the effects of the Depression took about a year to hit Seattle and the rest of Washington state, but when it did, it struck harder than in many places. Whereas the national unemployment rate eventually topped out at roughly 25 percent, Washington's average rate in 1933 was 33 percent, and it was even higher in many of the larger cities, including Seattle.[12] Encampments for displaced workers sprung up across the Puget Sound region. The most notable was a shantytown on the tideflats adjacent to the Port of Seattle. One of many "Hoovervilles" named for the president who insisted the downturn would be short-lived, the encampment near the present-day SoDo area was created from scrounged-up discarded items and housed hundreds of the hardest-hit men who ended up surviving off soup kitchens and other tapped-out charitable organizations.

Across the nation, professional sports leagues and the athletes competing in them often became charity cases as well. The most popular sport of the day, Major League Baseball, saw attendance decline by 35 percent from 1929 to 1933[13], and attendance at other sporting activities large and small dropped, too.

But rather than fade from focus, as might be expected when basic human survival is at stake, an interesting phenomenon occurred in the sporting world: The cathartic quality of such competitions became more apparent. Athletes became heroes because their chosen occupations offered a reprieve from reality. Sports became a vital part of society, and community members stepped up to make sure those two- or three-hour-long mental breaks they had become accustomed to continued. Sports, in turn, gave back financially by donating portions of gate receipts to charities.

In Seattle, the Washington Athletic Club played a large role in this sports-as-escapism movement. Several groups stepped in to help raise funds for the Seattle athletes vying for spots on the 1932 U.S. Olympic Team, and the club opened its doors as the athletes' training ground. Varnell did his part there, too, with several of his "Varnell Says" columns dedicated to seeing that, "Seattle's great athletes, men and women, swimmers and track and field performers, may have the opportunity to use their talents for Uncle Sam in the Olympic Games at Los Angeles. ... But Seattle has no fund with which to send these athletic greats to the final trials at which the Olympic team will be selected."[14]

Varnell's influence led to the Washington Athletic Club's selection as Olympic fundraising headquarters. The campaign was a success, and Seattle sent several athletes to the trials in Palo Alto, California, and New York City, after which the U.S. Olympic Committee covered the costs of those athletes who had qualified for the Games. At the forefront among those qualifiers was nineteen-year-old swimmer Helene Madison, who had completed almost all her training in the WAC's pool and at one point held more than twenty world records. Madison won three gold medals in Los Angeles, and on August 26, 1932, returned home to Seattle to the largest ticker-tape parade in the city's history to that point, with some 175,000 in attendance. Seattle's population that year was roughly 300,000.

Varnell remained close with his connections in Spokane, often returning to visit friends, family, and former colleagues. During one such trip, in June 1932, he gave a lecture on officiating at Gonzaga's summer coaching school, an event that also hosted seminars with former National Football League player Heartley "Hunk" Anderson. One year prior, Anderson had become head football coach at Notre Dame after Knute Rockne was killed in a plane crash. Gus Dorais—another former NFL player and, like Varnell, also a former head football coach at Gonzaga—also lectured at the coaching school.

The trip to Gonzaga was the second Varnell had taken east of the Cascades in a month. That May, he had crossed the Cascades to the Rockies via train to Missoula, Montana, where for the fifteenth consecutive year, he worked as an unpaid volunteer starter of the two day Montana state high school track meet. It was a tradition Varnell had started in 1916, when he lived some 300 miles closer, and one he would continue for three more decades. Many of Varnell's visits drew praise from *The Daily Missoulian*, including his trip in 1935: "With George Varnell firing the pistol for the start of the races … the Interscholastic will be efficiently handled as in the past, rolling along with speed and precision … [Varnell] is one of the best known, best liked, and most efficient athletic officials in the West."[15] The story was accompanied by a photo of a smiling Varnell, sharply dressed in suit jacket and striped bowtie, and the photo caption continued the praise: "[Varnell is] the most competent, popular and capable sports official in the West, who has given Montana satisfaction in his work on track, gridiron, and court."[16]

Such assignments offered no money, but at times they brought greater rewards. On one occasion, April 19, 1936, Varnell was the starter for the Silver Skis Race on Mount Rainier, which began at 10,000-foot-high Camp Muir and traveled down to Paradise Valley at 6,000 feet. Top skiers from across the world—including professional Hannes Schroll of Austria—were in attendance. Also in attendance, nestled among the thousands of spectators gathered near the two-story, wooden Paradise Inn, were nineteen-year-old Ginna Varnell, a third-year student at the University of Washington, and a twenty-four-year-old named Maurice "Mike" Spencer Dunn. He was the youngest of five children born to Arthur G. Dunn, a prominent Seattle businessman and half of the Ainsworth & Dunn team that owned and operated an eponymous salmon-packing company and several downtown piers. Mike Dunn, a former high school football player and UW student, again crossed paths with Ginna Varnell in September 1937, when both were in the wedding party of Bill Blethen (another of the publisher's sons) and Jane Calvert. Mike and Ginna were married some eight years later, on December 29, 1945, after Mike returned from a thirty-eight-month tour of duty as a naval lieutenant in Hawaii during World War II.

While Mike was in Hawaii, Ginna had worked in Seattle for the government as a mail censor. The newlyweds moved to the Dunn family's country property in North Seattle, which today is part of the nonprofit Dunn Gardens and on the National Register of Historic Places. Mike Dunn went on to a lifelong career at People's Bank. Ginna managed the household and was an active volunteer for numerous organizations, including serving as the librarian at her children's elementary school, Broadview. Her annual book talks at the Sunset Club were a popular attraction at the private women's organization.

YOGI

LIKE A COACH EVALUATING talent and a parent inspecting the performance of a cherished son, George Varnell watched the sleek cedar shells ply the waterway linking Lake Washington to Puget Sound. Each crisp, spring morning he did this, from the late 1920s to the early 1960s, observing with open heart the University of Washington rowers he later that day would report on. These were the same young men whose practice races he would officiate and after whose annual Class Day Regatta he would award each winner an oar-shaped, golden tiepin. Officially, Varnell was at Montlake Cut on assignment for *The Seattle Daily Times*. Unofficially, he was there as part of the squad.

Crew was one area of reporting where most readers, from casual browsers to diehard crew fans, agreed Varnell was on top of his game.

"George Varnell knew the men on the crews," said John "Maggie" Magnuson, a UW Crew member during Varnell's later years at *The Seattle Daily Times*.

> [He] knew where we went to high school, what we were ma-
> joring in, and whether our parents came to watch us row. He
> wrote what he experienced by being with us at the turnouts,
> races, and evening meals. He always asked what we were go-
> ing to do after college. How were we going to make a living, to
> apply what we were learning? Deep-thought questions for boys
> trying to focus on the next turnout or the next race or getting
> by the next final exam. He told me that in order to pay for
> college tuition for my future children I should save coins every
> day. He told me that he did that with dimes and paid for his
> daughter's college. I still do it to this day. My daughter's first
> year at university was paid for by the George Varnell theory.
> Now I am saving for her boy's tuitions. Every day when I drop
> a few coins in a large jar, I think of George Varnell.[1]

"He also traveled with us," said Tren Griffin, who along with his twin brother, Art, was a Husky coxswain from 1948-51. "Travel in those days was always by train: the Southern Pacific to Berkeley and the Milwaukee and New York Central to Poughkeepsie (the New York site that was, from 1895-1949, home of the U.S. Inter-collegiate Rowing Association's national championship). [Varnell] would sit with us, join our conversations, relate sport stories, give advice if asked, and was an enjoyable companion."[2] Griffin recalled one such trip when the team's train was passing through Ohio, and Coach Al Ulbrickson got locked in the bathroom. In a time when trains did not yet have sewer-collection systems and waste just dropped on the tracks below as the train kept a-rollin', Ulbrickson was trapped for several minutes while Varnell fussed about trying to help the coach. When the train's crew eventually unlocked the door, Ulbrickson emerged and told Varnell: "They are going to remember me in that town for a long time!"[3] Griffin also recalled the story of Varnell saving dimes for his daughter, Ginna, placing the coins in a large piggy bank he kept in his apartment. Varnell then would take the dimes and deposit them, as he had for years, into his bank branch located below his office at *The Times*.

John Wilcox, a UW rower in the late 1950s and early 1960s, has similar fond memories: "I knew [Varnell] about as well as an athlete can know a famous sportswriter. He was kind of a hero to many of us because we sensed that he loved our sport about as much as we did. We all

George Varnell's official Seattle Daily Times headshot. (The Associated Press via The Seattle Times)

knew he was attracted to the purity of our sport ... but most of all he was a kind and supportive gentleman, the sort, for instance, who would remember to have copies of particularly good *Seattle Times* photographs reproduced for our personal collections."[4]

Perhaps Varnell's most important—or at least most renowned—contributions to UW crew came in the summer of 1936. That June, he was on hand when the Husky rowers won the national championship in Poughkeepsie, defeating reigning champion California, as well as teams from Navy, Columbia, Cornell, Penn, and Syracuse. As the Husky varsity rowers crossed the line in front by a length to complete a UW sweep (its JV and freshmen teams had won earlier), Varnell watched from a VIP train car. In the car, as described by Daniel James Brown in his best-seller, *The Boys in the Boat*, "... Al Ulbrickson's mouth twitched reluctantly into something vaguely resembling a smile. ... George Pocock threw back his head and howled like a banshee. ... [And] George Varnell removed the well-masticated remains of his press credentials from his mouth."[5]

In July 1936, shortly after qualifying for that year's Olympics in Berlin, the Huskies were told they would have to cover their own costs to get to Germany. Covering such an expense—especially in the throes of the Great Depression—was unlikely, but the alternative was more painful. If UW could not fund its way, the runner-up and deep-pocketed University of Pennsylvania team surely could. The situation fired up UW supporters, including Varnell, who through his stories, personal connections, phone calls, and volunteerism helped direct a grass-roots effort to raise the funds to send the crew to the Olympics. At his paper, Royal Brougham did the same.

For all Varnell's efforts, *The Times* did not cover the cost of his travel to Berlin. *The P.I.*, however, paid for Brougham to go, although his stories never saw the light of day because *The P.I.* was in the beginning stages of a 103-day strike.

In the Berlin suburb of Grunau on August 14, 1936, the Husky eight, powered by a group of blue-collar students from Washington state—some of whom had gotten sick during the eight-day steamship trip across the Atlantic—staged a come-from-behind victory to win the gold medal by a few feet over second-place Italy and host Germany, which finished an ignominious third—all as a deflated Adolf Hitler looked on. Coxswain Bobby Moch had engineered yet another of his patented start-slow, finish-fast victories, which left Coach Ulbrickson limp.* The Husky oarsmen, rowing for their country, were in sync like some marvelous, mystical machine.

Now immortalized in Brown's book, it was one of the most stirring victories in the history of sports. *The Times* used coverage from the Associated Press to report the UW victory on its front page. Three days later, a group of Seattleites, including Varnell and Brougham, formed a committee to bring the Olympic Trials to Seattle in 1940 in advance of the Japan Olympics, which ultimately were canceled due to World War II.

Varnell's first story on the crew's inspiring Berlin victory came

---

* Moch, the son of a jeweler in Montesano, Washington, learned a family secret just before the team's departure for Germany when he opened a letter from his father: They were Jewish. The irony of a slight Jewish youth engineering a victory that was a slap in the face to Nazi Germany is one of the enduring revelations of Brown's book.

in an August 18 "Varnell Says" column: "With oars hung up by all divisions of Washington's navy, history records that the Purple and Gold sweep pullers enjoyed their most successful season in rowing annals. … What a glorious campaign the Huskies' crews turned in for 1936!"[6]

The year 1936 was a big one for Seattle sports outside the UW crew's victory. UW swimmer Jack Medica won three medals, including a gold, at the Olympics, and the U.S. men's basketball team, which included UW star Ralph Bishop, won a gold medal. The 7-1-1 Husky football team Varnell had covered all year made it to the Rose Bowl. Varnell, by then 55, officiated the January 1, 1937, game—the first time in a decade he had worked the big game.

The Husky loss to Pittsburgh in the 23rd Rose Bowl was Varnell's last time refereeing on college football's biggest stage, though he continued to officiate football games until 1946, the birth year of Varnell's first grandchild, Pat Dunn—named after his maternal grandfather, Patrick Henry Winston. Subsequent grandchildren—Dorothy (who died at a young age), Virginia (born in 1951), and Ned (born in 1952)—each stole a piece of Varnell's heart, and family memories still shared among the grandchildren show how Varnell embraced his grandfatherly role. Each Sunday, George and Liz would drive to North Seattle to spend the day with their daughter and family. Former athlete Varnell enjoyed the physical exertion of yardwork with his son-in-law, Mike Dunn, Varnell's yardwork clothes hanging in the front closet like a uniform in a locker. Varnell's grandchildren called him "Baba." Family lunch every Sunday was served in the Dunn home, often with vanilla ice cream, after George spent time working in the greencry around the house and tending to other projects. His grandchildren knew that if they temporarily left the table while eating their ice cream, it could well be gone when they got back. Baba would have hidden it as a joke; the children never seemed to tire of it. He also brought them spare material for drawing and writing from his newspaper office; these became lovingly known in the household as "Baba paper" and "Baba pencils."

THE OPENING WEEK of the 1939 college football season marked the return of Varnell's popular "guesser" column forecasting the outcome of upcoming West Coast games. Varnell secured a 4-3-1 record for the week, a feat depicted in a nearly half-page cartoon drawn by Sam Groff on the front page of Monday's sports section in *The Times*. The two-panel illustration shows each of mascots from three of the losing teams being tossed into washtubs, while in the second panel, "Yogi" Varnell, dressed in a sorcerer's robe, is chased by three steers. In the accompanying story, Varnell explained away his mediocre showing: "Wreckage from one of the daffiest weekends in Pacific Coast football history was washed up on the shore today. No football derby since the organization of the Pacific Coast Conference has been marked with such heavy casualties of favorites on opening day."[7] The guest guessers that week included Varnell's former Gonzaga star turned Seattle Rainiers manager, Bill Mulligan, and Washington state horse-racing pioneer Joe Gottstein. Varnell's guesser columns remained essentially the same—save for a permanent change in his byline from George Varnell to Yogi Varnell—each week during football season for the next two-plus decades.

The list of Seattle sports highlights that occurred during the years Varnell headed *The Times'* sports coverage is replete with memorable victories and heartbreaking losses. As a writer, an editor, or simply an enthusiastic spectator, Varnell was involved with each of the major assignments broken out into sections below:

———

With the help of stars such as George Archie, Edo Vanni, Jo-Jo White, Fred Hutchinson, and Ryne Duren, the Seattle Rainiers AAA baseball team won several Pacific Coast League titles in the 1940s and 1950s, including in 1955, when Hutchinson was the team's manager. Though the minor league club was not part of his beat, Varnell regularly attended Rainiers games at Sicks' Stadium and edited the stories, drawing on his expertise as a former stand-out baseball player.

———

In 1948, the University of Washington's four-man crew with coxswain, coached by George Pocock instead of Al Ulbrickson, defeated Switzerland and Denmark to win an Olympic gold medal at Henley-on-Thames in England, Pocock's home course. Neither Varnell nor anyone else from *The Seattle Daily Times* was in attendance. Varnell had, however, attended the Olympic Trials for the Varsity 8 in July on Lake Carnegie in Princeton, New Jersey, where the late-afternoon Varsity 8 race was reported live back to Seattle by Royal Brougham on KOMO Radio. Varnell wrote: "With 20 yards left the bow of the *Winlock Miller* was only a forward deck behind the *George Blair*. Two more strokes and the crews were separated by inches, but there was the finish line. Two more strokes and the Huskies shot their shell out in front, not by feet, but by yards. Had the Washington sprint been started sooner, the Huskies would have won the race."[8] The Olympic victory for the four-man plus coxswain crew helped persuade the state Legislature to fund a new crew facility, the Conibear Shellhouse, on the UW campus. That September, Varnell, Brougham, Pocock, and Ulbrickson were part of a panel of speakers, including UW freshman football head coach John Cherberg, gathered at The Arctic Club in Seattle to offer recaps of the Olympics. Cherberg would go on to serve as the state's lieutenant governor for thirty-two years.

———

One of the most successful collegiate basketball seasons in Seattle history occurred in 1953, with both Seattle University and the University of Washington men qualifying for the NCAA Tournament. As one might expect, Varnell was tasked to cover the Huskies, whom he had followed all year. UW's first tournament game was March 13 in front of 10,000 fans in Corvallis, Oregon, against Seattle University and its high-scoring all-American, five-foot-nine-

THE SEATTLE DAILY TIMES   FRIDAY, OCTOBER 14, 1938.

YOGI VARNELL PICKS WASHINGTON!—By Sam Groff

Yogi Varnell's football pick-em column, this one illustrated by Sam Groff, ran prominently each week in The Seattle Daily Times.

inch Johnny O'Brien. O'Brien scored a team-high 25 points, but Washington's Bob "Hooks" Houbregs scored an NCAA Tournament record 45, and the Husky defense smothered the Chieftains, 92-70. While Johnny O'Brien and his twin brother, Eddie, almost immediately signed deals with baseball's Pittsburgh Pirates, Houbregs and the Huskies went on to beat Santa Clara, 74-62, the next day to advance to the Final Four. Varnell followed the Huskies to Kansas City, Missouri, watching as Kansas overwhelmed Washington, 79-53, to move on to the championship game against Indiana. "Kansas simply pressed the life out of Washington's offense from the opening tipoff until the final gun," Varnell wrote in the next day's *Times*. "Any time a Husky got the ball he found a Kansas Jayhawk giving him little chance to pass with any degree of accuracy. While the Husky with the ball was being covered the other members of the team were anything but on the loose. The Kansas defense overlooked no one."[9] Houbregs scored 18 points, but fouled out early in the second half. Houbregs and the Huskies bounced back the following night in the consolation game against future Hall of Famer Bob Pettit and Louisiana State, winning 88-69 behind Houbregs's 42 points. Later in the month, Varnell noted, "The 1953 Washington basketball team ... was the greatest in Washington history. The figures prove it. Bob Houbregs hung up more records than any player in conference history. The Huskies had a won-and-lost record that tops all Washington teams. The Huskies (with a final record of 30-3) rated higher in national play than any previous Washington team."[10] The third-place finish still stands as the best finish in UW basketball history. When UW's Houbregs moved on to the NBA, Seattle U's Chieftains became the dominant college basketball team in Seattle for nearly two decades. The teams did not play each other to determine supremacy on the court. Still, from that 1953 season through to 1969, Seattle U made it to eleven NCAA Tournaments, its best showing coming in 1958, when, led by Elgin Baylor, it advanced to the championship game in Louisville, Kentucky, against the University of Kentucky. The Chieftains lost, 84-72.

*George Varnell was the volunteer starter for Montana's state high school
track meet for forty consecutive years. (Varnell family photo)*

———

In July 1958, still operating under sanctions imposed by the NCAA due to football recruiting violations, Husky Crew traveled behind the Iron Curtain to Moscow to race against boats from the Soviet Union. On July 19, on the choppy, Lake Washington-like waters of the Khimki Reservoir, the Husky boat pulled away from all competitors to easily win the 2,000-meter race. Though Varnell had covered crew all year long, *The Times* sent sports editor Georg Meyers to Moscow while Varnell stayed in the Northwest and covered Husky basketball. But Varnell was back on his beat when the team returned to Seattle, writing an end-of-season wrap-up. Of the historic trip to the Soviet Union, Ulbrickson told Varnell, "The Russians treated us like old friends."[11]

———

Varnell, who spent his days heaping praise on deserving college athletes, also was racking up accolades of his own. In 1938, *Times* management had named him an associate editor of the entire paper, the third employee ever given that honor. And, as he had for most of his career, Varnell also *made* the news on a regular basis. The aviophobic Varnell's first plane flight—reluctantly scheduled when he determined the train would not get him to Los Angeles in time for him to cover an important UCLA–UW basketball game—warranted a 10-inch, top-of-page story with pictures in the February 3, 1956, edition of *The Times*. "Air-Borne at Last," the headline read. The accompanying photo featured a grinning, seventy-three-year-old Varnell pointing to the sky in front of the plane's door as he boarded the Huskies's charter flight.

The following year, as he continued to scale back his sportswriting duties, Varnell was one of three honorees at the inaugural Ray T. Rocene Sportsman of the Year banquet at the Hotel Florence in Missoula, Montana. The event's official program praised Varnell for his 40 consecutive years as a starter for Montana's state prep track meet. George and Liz Varnell and the other two hon-

George Varnell rests his arms on the shoulders of friend Johnny Katsaros at George and Liz's 50th wedding anniversary party in 1961. (Varnell family photo)

orees—sportswriter Rocene and Bernie Bierman, a former Montana football coach who later coached the University of Minnesota to five national championships—sat at the head table and dined on Rocene Ribbing Roast, Rye-land bread, Green String Deanes, and other items from a pun-filled menu.

During halftime of the December 3, 1960, UW-BYU basketball game at Edmundson Pavilion, Greater Seattle, Inc. awarded Varnell its First Citizen in Sports trophy. Three weeks later, Varnell was Rose Bowl-bound aboard a seventeen-car Northern Pacific Railway train when it derailed near Puyallup, Washington, injuring twelve people. Varnell was unhurt and made it to the game to watch the Huskies, behind quarterback Bob Schloredt, upset top-ranked Minnesota, 17-7. Varnell's game recap focused on Coach Jim Owens's strategy. "Owens … played this game in cagey fashion. … [He] made substitutions with a generous hand. Thus, when the going got rough, he had athletes to call in from the bench to face the Gophers with no reduction in efficiency."[12]

Perhaps nowhere was Varnell's popularity more obvious than at his and Liz's fiftieth wedding anniversary party, held July 12, 1961, at the Seattle Golf Club. The Winstons, the Blethens and several other well-known families all had received gold-adorned invitations, their names recorded in a multipage registry adjacent to their gifts to the golden anniversary couple. Others came from cities Varnell had frequented on his press, and life, assignments over the years, including Corvallis, San Francisco, and Spokane. Many who could not make it sent telegrams, including Washington

Congressman Thomas Pelly. Family scrapbooks contain dozens of snapshots of the event—George bald, bespectacled, and wearing a full suit with white shirt and striped tie, and Liz in a light-colored, floral print dress, both posing for pictures with many attendees.

Despite all the dignitaries in attendance that day—Seattle's hottest of the year at 97 degrees—Varnell's most treasured guest was one whose name would not ring a bell with anyone outside the smallest of familial circles. The guest, Johnny Katsaros, for years had run the concession stand outside Hec Edmundson Pavilion on the University of Washington campus. Varnell asked his grandson, fourteen-year-old Pat, to wait in the doorway to watch for Katsaros and make certain he and his wife were properly seated, and every grandchild had his or her picture taken with Katsaros.

"I was kind of hoping it would be a small party, maybe even a quiet dinner at home," Varnell told *Times* writer John J. Reddin for a front-page story about the couple's anniversary. "But my daughter Virginia wouldn't hear of it. She has taken charge, and things have really gotten out of hand."[13] The rest of Reddin's story read like a recap of Varnell's career. At seventy-eight, the "bald, perpetually sun-tanned dean of Pacific Northwest sportswriters" still was working, Reddin wrote. "Varnell is one of the most punctual persons we've ever known—also one of the kindest and most accommodating. He arrives at his desk in the sports department promptly at 5:45 o'clock each morning, winter or summer. At noon, he walks to the Washington Athletic Club, where he takes a steam bath but seldom eats lunch. Varnell spends each weekday afternoon at the University of Washington covering the practice session of whatever sport is in season—football, basketball, baseball, crew, swimming, tennis, and the less-glamorous minor sports. Consequently, 'Coach,' as he is known affectionately by many generations of college students, is the most highly regarded non-alumnus at the university."[14]

In March 1966, George and Liz Varnell returned to Spokane for George's induction into the Inland Empire Sports Hall of Fame, which took place during halftime of the State Class B basketball championship game in the Spokane Coliseum. "It was great to

Frank Blethen Sr., left, hands George Varnell a retirement gift as Liz Varnell watches at George's retirement ceremony from The Seattle Times in 1966. (Varnell family photo)

have George Varnell back in his 'home town,'" wrote *The Spokane Daily Chronicle* sports editor Bob Johnson. "[Varnell] was as delighted as a teen-ager at the honors accorded him."[15] Over dinner at the Davenport Hotel, George told Johnson a story the Varnell family already knew by heart—about how, one day while he was at work, Liz called him and casually inserted a question about moving:

"Would you want to move to another house, George?"

"I suppose so," was the reply.

Liz called back a few minutes later.

"Would you mind living in an apartment?"

"I don't mind," George said.

Near the end of his shift, George received a final phone call from his wife:

"When you come home, come to [a new address]. We've moved."[16]

IN APRIL 1966, THE UNIVERSITY OF WASHINGTON CREW raced its interclass regatta, and the following month, the school named a shell after Varnell.

In June, with her father ailing at home in his Roy Street apartment, Ginna Varnell Dunn traveled to Syracuse, New York, site of the Intercollegiate Rowing Association championships, to christen the George Varnell shell with water brought in a jug from Lake Washington.

*Ginna Varnell christens a shell named after her father
in June 1966 in Syracuse, New York, as University of Washington
crew members and head coach Matthew Fillip "Fil" Leanderson,
at right in sunglasses, look on. (The Associated Press)*

Varnell's official retirement date from *The Seattle Times* was September 1, 1966. The paper's staff—led by Frank Blethen Sr., the former UW coxswain—had thrown him a party two weeks prior in the paper's cafeteria. George and Liz both attended and were given gifts, including a poster-size editorial cartoon depicting Varnell lying atop a stack of encyclopedias casually writing a story. There was a typewriter on his lap, and he was dressed in his prognosticating "Yogi" outfit. Three days later, writer Reddin paid tribute to his colleague:

"For the first time in [decades], 'Yogi' Varnell will be absent from his familiar perch in the University of Washington Stadium press box. Somehow, things won't seem the same."[17]

THE FINISH LINE

T IS LATE MARCH 2021, an overcast Saturday morning—48 degrees and windy on the mildly choppy Montlake Cut. Native Americans once called this section of the Lake Washington ship canal *sxWatSadweehL,* "carry a canoe," because for centuries that is what they had to do to travel through this area and continue their transport of resources from the hills east of modern-day Seattle to the saltwater-side trading posts on Puget Sound.

Countless people line the narrow passageway's north and south shores, while others gather on the landmark drawbridge spanning the waterway. The shovels, dynamite, and machinery of early white settlers, and the backs of immigrant Chinese laborers, had worked to turn this muddy isthmus into a shipping canal. Today, commerce prospers, together with recreation, as boats float freely between Lake Washington to the east and Lake Union to the west.

*Legendary racing shell builder George Pocock hands the large George M. Varnell Trophy
to University of Washington coxswain Bob Witter after the Class Day Regatta in Seattle
in 1953. To the right of Witter are rowers Guy Harper and Keith Reilly. Immediately behind
Pocock is UW head coach Al Ulbrickson. A smiling George Varnell is at left in the middle of
the boat, with his arm resting on his right leg. (The Seattle Daily Times)*

The spectators are here for the 120th edition of the University of Washington's Class Day Regatta, intersquad races that launch the spring season for the men's and women's rowing programs. Spectator boats, including small cruise ships with rails overflowing with fans, sit at each end of the cut, every passenger hoping to catch a glimpse of the squads vying for victory in their racing shells. Among the day's highlights is the 2,000-meter men's eight. The winning team gains bragging rights; its coxswain earns a celebratory toss in the lake; and the victorious class gets its name permanently etched into the sizable, double-handled George M. Varnell Trophy. Former UW rowers return to the race each year to find their names on the trophy to show family and friends.

The entrance to Portage Bay marks the finish line for the racers. The finish line for the trophy's namesake had come on February 4, 1967, after a stay in a Seattle hospital—some 2,000 miles and 84½ years away from his starting blocks in Chicago.

The George M. Varnell Trophy is awarded each year to the winner of the 2,000-meter men's eight crew race during the University of Washington's Class Day Regatta. (Rodrigo DeMedeiros)

ACROSS THE SNOW-CAPPED CASCADES from which the waters of the Montlake Cut originate, the decades-long success of the men's basketball program that George Varnell helped establish at Gonzaga University in Spokane has led to dramatic changes on campus. Many believe basketball saved the school. Since the Bulldogs' first appearance in the Elite Eight round of the 1999 NCAA Tournament, applications have steadily risen, as has the size of the school's endowment fund. Several impressive new buildings have been constructed, including a splendid $27 million, 6,000-seat basketball arena that's always sold out and a 51,000-square-foot athletic practice facility that includes a gym, weight and film rooms, study spaces, and meeting rooms. The school's first coach, Varnell, certainly would be proud. For the record, his teams—including the official 1908-09 team and the 1907-08 unofficial one—won 82.6 percent of their games.

Meanwhile, Gonzaga's once-vaunted football program—which produced two Pro Football Hall of Famers: Ray Flaherty (1926), head coach of the Washington Redskins, and Tony Canadeo (1941) of the Green Bay Packers—was a casualty of World War II. Varnell's official 10-4-1 record and 71 percent winning record during his three years as Gonzaga's football coach leave him third all-time among those who lasted more than one season, and ahead of the school's most famous coach, Hall of Famer Charles E. "Gus" Dorais (20-13-3 record; .597 winning percentage). The football stadium Varnell broke ground on in 1922 was razed in 1949.

AN EASY MILE OR SO WALK west from Gonzaga across busy Division Street stands the 12,000-seat Spokane Arena, home ice for the Chiefs minor league hockey team and less-regular host to high school and college basketball games, as well as touring comedians, musical acts, and motorsports. Inside the arena's front doors on its newly remodeled concourse exists the usual modern array of teller

George Varnell's exhibit at the Inland Northwest Sports Hall of Fame
in the Spokane Arena. (Spokane Sports Commission/Sammie Ragan)

machines, dining and drinking options, as well as a wall featuring dozens of inset, glass-covered displays containing photographs and other memorabilia of those enshrined in the Inland Northwest Sports Hall of Fame. George Varnell is here, alongside other Spokane-area sports notables: Joe Albi; Bobby Brett, owner of the Spokane Indians and brother of Hall of Fame baseball player George; Don Kardong, the former Olympic runner who founded Spokane's popular Lilac Bloomsday Run.

At the top of a wall immediately above the Hall of Fame's centerpiece, Varnell's tribute includes a framed photograph of the inductee and a summary of his accomplishments. The display is fronted by the well-worn silver whistle Varnell used for each of the record eight Rose Bowls he officiated.

DURING THE FALL OF 2020, some fifty-three years after Varnell's death, an older gentleman is randomly spotted taking a brisk morning walk through a neighborhood park in Tacoma, Washington, his head sporting a purple ball cap with a large gold "W" on its crown. What is his connection with the University of Washington? A quick conversation provides the answer. The walker is eighty-six-year-old Mel Kobel—"Mudder" to those who knew him from his days as a sub-10-second 100-yard dasher on the Husky track team in the 1950s. When Varnell's name comes up in conversation, Kobel's jaw drops, his mouth opens, and enthusiasm comes out: "I knew George Varnell really well. He was at our track practices all the time. Such a nice guy who was a great writer because he always treated his sources as equals." Through a light mist, the conversation continues. Stories flow about Varnell's sharp clothing, and how he once had caught Kobel vomiting behind a grandstand after a blistering training session. The next day, at nearly the same time, Kobel is back at the Tacoma park, a folded sheet of paper peeking above the edge of his jacket pocket. The paper is filled with handwritten remembrances of Varnell:

> He observed our practices, talked to us, asking us questions about our coach, asked about injuries and treatment. For many years, I read his columns and admired his ability to report U of W sports in realistic terms. He brought out a human element of real athletes and their effort and attitude, understanding what it means to be part of a unified group. George used the terminology of each sport he covered as if he had been involved and gone through the same learning curve. Now I know the reason: He had been!

IN THESE PLACES AND OTHERS, George Varnell's substantial legacy as an athlete, coach, and sportswriter still is felt. His accomplishments were in danger of becoming little more than footnotes and faded ephemera until his descendants discovered a trove of old columns and started digging. They concluded that a man who participated in hundreds of significant historical moments, witnessed and recorded thousands more, and used his pen and persona to help people become stars should not be forgotten. Were medals awarded for such a life as his, Varnell clearly would have won a gold for coaching, complimenting, and complementing others, yet rarely speaking of any achievements of his own.

CHRONOLOGY

1882

George Marshall Varnell is born on August 10 in Chicago, Illinois.

1898

His father, Harry "Prince Hal" Varnell, dies on September 12 at age forty-seven.

1899

Enrolls at Lewis Institute in Chicago, where he competes in five sports.

1902

Graduates from high school at Lewis Institute; begins attending Lewis Institute's School of Arts in Chicago.

1904

Graduates from Lewis Institute's School of Arts in Chicago; competes in two events at the St. Louis Olympics; plays football for Amos Alonzo "A.A." Stagg at the University of Chicago.

1905

Leaves University of Chicago; enrolls at Kentucky University and stars on the football team.

1906

Marries Katherine Emmal in Nicholasville, Kentucky.

1907

Moves to Spokane, Washington, to work for the Spokane Amateur Athletic Club; plays baseball and football for the club, and coaches its football team; moonlights as Gonzaga College's basketball and football coach.

1908

Begins job as head of athletic department at Gonzaga College in Spokane, Washington; resurrects the school's football teams and becomes the sport's head coach; officially establishes the basketball team and becomes its head coach; becomes sportswriter for *The Spokane Daily Chronicle*.

1910

Becomes sports editor at *The Spokane Daily Chronicle*.

1911

Marries Martha Elizabeth Winston at her family's home in Spokane, Washington, on July 12.

1916

Only child, daughter Virginia Elizabeth, is born on November 3 in Spokane, Washington.

1919

Referees first of a record eight Rose Bowl games in Pasadena, California.

1922

Dubbed "The Walter Camp of the West" by *Sunset* magazine.

1923

Elected to the National Football Rules Committee.

1925

Moves across the state to Seattle, Washington, for a sportswriting job at *The Seattle Daily Times*, with a focus on the University of Washington crew and other collegiate sports.

1927

Named sports editor of *The Seattle Daily Times*.

1936

Helps raise funds for University of Washington's "Boys in the Boat" crew to attend Olympics in Germany, where the team wins a gold medal.

1937

Referees final Rose Bowl game.

1938

Given honorary title of associate editor of *The Seattle Daily Times;* launches popular "Yogi Varnell" football prediction column in *The Seattle Daily Times*.

1946

Retires from refereeing.

1960

Named Seattle's First Citizen in Sports.

1966

Inducted into the Inland Empire Sports Hall of Fame; retires from *The Seattle Daily Times*.

1967

Dies on February 4, at the age of eighty-four, in Seattle.

NOTES

Chapter 1: The Fall Before the Rise

1. Pierre de Coubertin. *Olympic Memoirs*. Reprinted by the LA84 Foundation http://library.la84.org/OlympicInformationCenter/OlympicReview/1977/ore111/ore111n.pdf (accessed December 11, 2015).
2. Jody Sowell. "St. Louis vs. Chicago: An Olympic Rivalry," *History Happens Here: The Missouri History Museum's Blog*, June 29, 2012, www.historyhappenshere.org/node/7250 (accessed July 14, 2016).
3. "Louisiana Purchase Exposition Not To Be Thrown Open To The World Until 1904," *The Evening Times*, January 17, 1902, p. A1.
4. Jason Kelly. "Hyde Park's Olympic History," *University of Chicago Magazine*, May-June 2009, http://magazine.uchicago.edu/0906/chicago_journal/olympic_history.shtml (accessed on July 10, 2016).
5. Bill Mallon. *The 1904 Olympic Games: Results for All Competitors in All Events, with Commentary*. Jefferson, N.C.: McFarland and Company, 1999, p. 106.

Chapter 2: Son of a Prince

1. "Sports Down a Raid: Varnell's Gamblers Give the Federation a Black Eye," *Chicago Tribune*, September 19, 1894, p. 5.
2. Donald L Miller. *City of the Century: The Epic of Chicago and the Making of America*. New York: Simon & Schuster Paperbacks, 1996, p. 509.
3. *History of Chicago and Souvenir of the Liquor Interest: The Nation's Choice for the Great Exposition, 1893*. Chicago: Belgravia Publishing, 1893.
4. Emmett Dedmon. *Fabulous Chicago: A Great City's History and People*. Garrett County Press Digital, ebook, 2012.
5. Archibald Grove ed. *The New Review*. London: William Heinemann, 1894, p. 568.
6. "Sports Down a Raid: Varnell's Gamblers Give the Federation a Black Eye," *Chicago Tribune*, September 19, 1894, p. 5.
7. Ibid.
8. "Police Raid a Gambling-House," *Chicago Tribune*, April 25, 1893, p. 6.
9. Letter from Harry A. Varnell to John Muir, January 25, 1863, John Muir Correspondence, University of the Pacific.
10. Ibid.
11. Ibid.
12. Victor Robinson ed. *Medical Review of Reviews*. Boston Medical Library, 1918. p. 612.
13. Ibid.
14. Ibid., p. 613.
15. Ibid., p. 616.
16. "The Lordly Pay-rolls," *Chicago Tribune*, February 5, 1887, p. 9.
17. "Extravagant Varnell," *Chicago Tribune*, February 19, 1887, p. 1.
18. "The Special Grand Jury," *Chicago Tribune*, March 8, 1887, pp. 1-2.
19. "Harry Varnell's 'Boodle,'" *Chicago Tribune*, December 4, 1887, p 9.

20. Ibid.
21. "Home from Joliet," *Chicago Tribune*, February 11, 1890, p. 1.
22. Ibid.
23. "Pool Rooms Raided," *The Chicago Inter Ocean*, November 7, 1895, p. 1.
24. "Death of Harry Varnell," *Chicago Tribune*, September 13, 1898, p. 10.
25. Ibid.
26. Ibid.
27. "The 'Good-Fellow' Politician," *The Pantagraph* (Bloomington, Illinois), September 16, 1898, p. 4.
28. "Died With Boots On," *The Chicago Inter Ocean*, April 30, 1899, p. 25.
29. "Now is Bishop Morrison," *Chicago Daily Tribune*, February 23, 1899, p. 10.
30. Agness J. Kaufman, "Historical Sketch of Lewis Institute," Illinois Institute of Technology, http://archives.iit.edu/lewis/ (accessed May 6, 2016).
31. *Lewis Institute Sixth Annual Register.* Chicago, 1902, p. 13.
32. "Athletes Combine Pledges and Games," *The Chicago Inter Ocean*, June 28, 1903, p. 13.

Chapter 3: America's Games

1. Robin Lester. *Stagg's University.* Champaign, Illinois: University of Illinois Press, 1999, p 44.
2. Ibid, pp. 9-10.
3. Rich Cohen. *Monsters: The 1985 Chicago Bears and the Wild Heart of Football.* New York: Farrar, Straus and Giroux, 2013, p. 37.
4. "Hogenson has cast his lot with Chicago," *Detroit Free Press*, July 13, 1904, p. 3.
5. "Hogenson Enters U. of C.," *Chicago Daily Tribune*, July 12, 1904, p. 8.
6. "Untitled newspaper clipping," *Oshkosh Daily Northwestern*, July 12, 1904, p. 2.
7. Ibid.
8. Lester, p. 52.
9. "Athletes Combine Pledges and Games," *The Chicago Inter Ocean*, June 28, 1903, p. 13.
10. "Rose Hurling Discus Beyond World's Mark," *Detroit Free Press*, August 28, 1904, p. 11.
11. Susan Brownell ed. *The 1904 Anthropology Days and Olympic Games: Sport, Race, and American Imperialism.* Lincoln, Nebraska: University of Nebraska Press, 2008, p. 43.
12. "The Olympic Games at St. Louis," *St. Louis Post-Dispatch*, August 28, 1904, p. 43.
13. Charles J.P. Lucas. *The Olympic Games 1904.* St. Louis: Woodward & Tiernan, 1905. p. 53.
14. Ibid. p. 78.
15. "Another World's Record Goes," *The Springfield Republican*, September 2, 1904.

Chapter 4: Marooned

1. *The President's Report: July, 1904 – July, 1905.* Chicago: The University of Chicago Press, 1906, p. 98.
2. Robin Lester. *Stagg's University.* Champaign, Illinois: University of Illinois Press, 1999, p 17.
3. Ibid, p. 55.

4. "Football Coach Contract of 1901," Michigan Athletic Association, http://bentley. umich.edu/athdept/images/yost_contract_1901.pdf, (accessed August 19, 2016).
5. "Football in the limelight," *The Illinois State Journal*, September 19, 1904.
6. "Michigan 28, Chicago 0," *The New York Times*, November 27, 1903. http://query.ny-times.com/mem/archive-free/pdf?res=9E01E3D81039E333A25754C2A9679D-946297D6CF (accessed August 14, 2016).
7. Edward S. Jordan, "Buying Football Victories," *Collier's Weekly*, November 11, 1905, p. 19.
8. Ibid.
9. Ibid, p. 20.
10. Amos Alonzo Stagg, "New Men," *A.A. Stagg Papers*, Box 24, Folder 3, 4687, Special Collections Research Center, University of Chicago Library.
11. Amos Alonzo Stagg, "General Defense," *A. A. Stagg Papers*, Box 30, Folder 8, 4688-4693, Special Collections Research Center, University of Chicago Library.
12. Ibid.
13. Ibid.
14. "Maroons Have Hard Schedule," *The Chicago Inter Ocean*, August 18, 1904.
15. "Eckersall in Form," *The Chicago Inter Ocean*, September 20, 1904, p. 4.
16. "Stagg gives up hope of winning," *The Minneapolis Journal*, September 21, 1904, p. 18.
17. Ibid.
18. "Englewood Too Light For The Maroon Team," *The Chicago Inter Ocean*, September 22, 1904, p. 4.
19. Ibid.
20. "North Siders Hold Maroons To Low Score," *The Chicago Inter Ocean*, September 29, 1904, p. 4.
21. Raymond Schmidt. *Shaping College Football: The Transformation of an American Sport, 1919-1930*. Syracuse, New York: Syracuse University Press, 2007, p. 9.
22. "Stagg Talks of Desertion," *Davenport Daily Republican*, September 29, 1904, p. 5.
23. "Deadly Work of Football in 1904," *Omaha World-Herald*, January 1, 1905.
24. "Painted Ball Will Be Used," *St. Louis Post-Dispatch*, October 16, 1904, p. 36.
25. "Baseball Mention," *Oshkosh Daily Northwestern*, January 7, 1905, p. 13.
26. "Chicago Loses Athletes," *The Des Moines Register*, January 29, 1905, p. 10.
27. "Defeat College Swimmers," *The Chicago Inter Ocean*, February 5, 1905, p. 9.
28. *The Purple and Gold: Volume XXII*. Auburn, New York: Chi Psi Fraternity, 1904, p. 170.
29. Ibid, p. 348.

Chapter 5: His New Kentucky Home

1. "Kentucky Team Wins," *The Dallas Morning News*, November 11, 1905.
2. "Kentucky University Downs Austin Team and Goes After Dallas," *The Lexington Leader*, November 11, 1905.
3. "Kentucky Team Wins," *The Dallas Morning News*, November 11, 1905.
4. "Kentucky University Downs Austin Team and Goes After Dallas," *The Lexington Leader*, November 11, 1905.
5. Ibid.

6. "Signal Welcome for K.U. Eleven," *The Lexington Herald*, November 16, 1905.
7. Ibid.
8. Gregory Kent Stanley. *Before Big Blue: Sports at the University of Kentucky 1880-1940*. Lexington, Kentucky: University of Kentucky Press, 1996, p. 29.
9. "34 to a Goose Egg," *The Lexington Leader*, November 5, 1905.
10. "Schacht Come Back," *The Lexington Leader*, November 28, 1905, p. 2.
11. Ibid.
12. Ibid.
13. "Crimson Close A Brilliant Season," *The Lexington Leader*, December 1, 1905, p. 7.
14. "Engagements of Interest," *The Lexington Herald*, February 25, 1906.
15. "Social-Personal," *The Lexington Leader*, March 4, 1906, p. 16.
16. "Organize Many Amateur Leagues," *The Chicago Inter Ocean*, February 4, 1906, p. 15.
17. "Informal Luncheon," *The Lexington Herald*, July 22, 1906.
18. "Surprise," *The Lexington Leader*, August 17, 1906, p. 1.
19. Ibid.
20. Ibid.
21. "Society," *The Lexington Herald*, June 30, 1907, p. 3.

Chapter 6: As Seen in Spokane

1. "Spokane Burnt," *The Seattle Post-Intelligencer*, August 5, 1889, p. 1.
2. Tony and Suzanne Bamonte. *Spokane: Our Early History—Under All Is The Land*. Spokane, Washington: Tornado Creek, 2012, p. 95.
3. "World of Sport," *The Spokane Press*, December 1, 1904, p. 3.
4. "Athletic Club is Opened," *The Spokane Press*, June 30, 1904, p. 3.
5. "May Coach the S.A.A.C. Team," *The Spokane Daily Chronicle*, July 22, 1907, p. 5.
6. "In Swift Twists," *The Spokane Daily Chronicle*, July 27, 1907, p. 5.
7. "Ballgame Was a Swatfest," *The Spokane Daily Chronicle*, July 29, 1907, p. 5.
8. "Choose Varnell as Physical Director," *The Spokane Daily Chronicle*, August 15, 1907, p. 5.
9. "To Be Advisor of Athletics," *The Spokane Daily Chronicle*, August 28, 1907, p. 5.
10. Ibid.
11. "Condition Tells on Club," *The Spokane Daily Chronicle*, October 21, 1907, p. 5.
12. "Big Football Games Today," *The Spokane Daily Chronicle*, October 26, 1907, p. 5.
13. "Makeshift Team Loses," *The Spokane Daily Chronicle*, October 28, 1907, p. 4.
14. "Take Down the Bars," *The Spokane Daily Chronicle*, November 13, 1907, p. 5.
15. "Seattle is Arrogant; Expects Easy Victory," *The Spokane Daily Chronicle*, November 26, 1907, p. 5.
16. Ibid.
17. "Seattle Team Beats Club," *The Spokane Daily Chronicle*, November 29, 1907, p. 5.
18. "Varnell Quits Spokane Athletic Club Cold," *The Seattle Daily Times*, December 8, 1907, p. 18.

Chapter 7: Gonzaga

1. "Gonzaga Proved Light," *The Spokesman-Review*, January 30, 1908, p. 11.
2. "S.A.A.C. Class Team is Expelled from League," *The Spokane Daily Chronicle*, Feb-

ruary 19, 1908, p. 6.

3. "Gonzaga to Have No Football Team," *The Spokane Daily Chronicle*, October 23, 1907, p. 5.

4. Bob Kirlin, "Gonzaga University Football," a personal report presented to Gonzaga University, 1981.

5. John J. Reddin, "Golden-Wedding Bells Ring For 'Coach' and 'Mother,' *The Seattle Daily Times*, July 9, 1961, p. 19.

6. "Gonzaga Eleven Shows Form," *The Spokane Daily Chronicle*, October 12, 1908, p. 18.

7. "Gonzaga Opens Fast," *The Spokane Press*, October 23, 1908, p. 6.

8. "Varnell Gonzaga Hero," *The Spokesman-Review*, October 1908.

9. "W.S.C. Winner Over Gonzaga," *The Spokane Daily Chronicle*, December 19, 1908, p. 4.

10. "Gonzaga Won Game From Club," *The Spokane Daily Chronicle*, January 2, 1909, p. 5.

11. "Gonzaga Wins, 26 To 8," *The Spokane Press*, January 8, 1909, p. 6.

12. "Gonzaga Plays A Great Game," *The Spokane Daily Chronicle*, January 13, 1909, p. 5.

13. "Gonzaga Boys Prove Mettle," *The Spokane Press*, January 30, 1909, page 6.

14. "Gonzaga Beats Whitman," *The Spokesman-Review*, February 12, 1909, p. 13.

Chapter 8: Daily Chronicles

1. Ralph E. Dyar, *News for an Empire: The Story of The Spokesman-Review of Spokane, Washington, and of the Field It Serves*, Caldwell, Idaho: Caxton Printers, 1952.

2. IXL Clothing advertisement, *The Spokane Daily Chronicle*, September 28, 1908, p. 7.

3. Harry Missildine, "Twice Over Lightly: George Says It's True, All Right," *The Spokesman-Review*, January 24, 1960.

4. "Tacoma Comment on Game," *The Wenatchee Daily World*, December 30, 1910, p. 8.

5. "Referee George Varnell," *The Wenatchee Daily World*, December 27, 1910, p. 1.

6. Samuel A. Ashe, Stephen B. Weeks, and Charles L. Van Noppen, editors. *Biographical History of North Carolina: From Colonial Times to Present*, Greensboro, North Carolina: Charles L. Van Noppen, 1905, p. 453.

7. Ibid.

8. "Bridge or Children," *The Spokane Daily Chronicle*, June 14, 1933, p. 11.

9. "Miss Elizabeth Winston To Be Bride Of George Varnell," *The Spokane Daily Chronicle*, June 14, 1911, p. 14.

10. "Washington And Oregon Elevens Battle To Tie," *The Seattle Post-Intelligencer*, November 5, 1916, p. 1.

11. George Varnell, "Varnell Deplores Loss Of Coach Dobie," *The (University of Washington) Daily*, December 13, 1916.

12. "Rothrock, Chronicle City Editor, Is Killed In Office By Assassin," *The Spokesman-Review*, April 25, 1912, p. 6.

13. "Odd Grid Incident Recalled by Varnell," *The Spokane Daily Chronicle*, October 26, 1936, p. 14.

14. "Big Game Referee Travels 1100 Miles," *The (University of Washington) Daily*, November 4, 1915.

15. "Golden Bear Crushed Beyond Recognition by Dobie's Washington Indians," *Oak-*

land Tribune, November 7, 1915.

16. "Hit That Line!" *The Spokane Daily Chronicle*, February 9, 1924, p. 9.

17. G.B. Foster, "Interesting Westerners," *Sunset*, December 1922, pp. 26-27.

18. Ibid.

19. George M. Varnell, "Clipping Hit Hard: Penalty Is Increased," *The Seattle Daily Times*, September 5, 1925, p. S2.

20. George M. Varnell, "The Try-At-Point," *The Seattle Daily Times*, December 14, 1926, p. S1.

21. "M.A.A.C. Asks Varnell To Be Its Manager," *The Bulletin*, December 6, 1924, p. 2.

Chapter 9: Good *Times* in Seattle

1. Bob Johnson, "Varnell Returns 'Home,'" *The Spokane Daily Chronicle*, March 8, 1966, p. 11.

2. John C. Hughes, *Pressing On: Two Family-Owned Newspapers in the 21st Century*, Olympia, Washington: Office of the Secretary of State, 2015, p. 26.

3. Ibid.

4. "Joins Times' Staff," *The Seattle Daily Times*, January 4, 1925, p. S3.

5. "Handball Tourney For Association Players," *The Seattle Daily Times*, January 18, 1925, p. S3.

6. George M. Varnell, "Rangy Oarsmen Make Up Squad For Two Boats," *The Seattle Daily Times*, March 6, 1925, p. S1.

7. George M. Varnell, "Shells Arrive On Same Train As 'W' Oarsmen," *The Seattle Daily Times*, June 10, 1925, p. S1.

8. Emmett Watson, "Royal Brougham Was More Than Just Another Name on a Downtown Street Sign," *The Seattle Times*, July 27, 1999, (http://community.seattletimes.nwsource.com/archive/?date=19990727&slug=2973996), accessed on December 26, 2017.

9. R.E. McKee, "They Never Quit," *The Seattle Daily Times*, November 14, 1945, p. 6.

10. Dave Eskenazi, "Wayback Machine: The Washington Athletic Club," *SportspressNW.com*, October 29, 2013, http://sportspressnw.com/2166466/2013/wayback-machine-the-washington-athletic-club (accessed December 26, 2017).

11. Ibid.

12. James Gregory, "Economics and Poverty," *The Great Depression in Washington State*, 2009, http://depts.washington.edu/depress/economics_poverty.shtml#_ednref3 (accessed December 28, 2017).

13. Andrea Adelson, "Sports Were Affected during the Great Depression," *The Orlando Sentinel*, January 20, 2009, http://articles.orlandosentinel.com/2009-01-20/sports/sportseconomy20_1_american-sports-history-new-deal-millions-of-americans (accessed December 28, 2017).

14. George M. Varnell, "Varnell Says: Olympic Funds Promised: Junior Chamber of Commerce Backs Seattle Stars," *The Seattle Daily Times*, May 30, 1932, p. 12.

15. "Veteran Officials In Charge Of Meet Under Way Today," *The Daily Missoulian*, May 16, 1935, sourced from clipping in family scrapbook.

16. Ibid.

Chapter 10: Yogi

1. John Magnuson, "Rowing and the Boys in the Boat" report, 2015 and author interviews, December 2018.
2. Author interviews with J. Trenholme Griffin, March 2018.
3. Ibid.
4. John Wilcox, email to Ned Dunn, March 18, 2010.
5. Daniel James Brown, *The Boys in the Boat: Nine Americans and Their Epic Quest for Gold at the 1936 Berlin Olympics*. New York: Penguin Books, 2013, p. 272.
6. George M. Varnell, "Varnell Says: Huskies Successful; They Won Eight Times; No More to Capture," *The Seattle Daily Times*, August 18, 1936, p. 18.
7. George M. Varnell, "Upsets Feature Opening Games," *The Seattle Daily Times*, October 2, 1939, p. 15.
8. George M. Varnell, "Bear Eight Topples U.W. by Split-Second," *The Seattle Daily Times*, July 3, 1948, p. 8.
9. George M. Varnell, "Huskies Suffer Worst Loss In Dye's Three-Year Reign," *The Seattle Daily Times*, March 18, 1953, p. 30.
10. George M. Varnell, "'53 Husky Five Was Best," *The Seattle Daily Times*, March 29, 1953, p. 50.
11. George M. Varnell, "Huskies Paid a Debt With Win over Russ Crew—Ulbrickson," *The Seattle Daily Times*, July 20, 1958, p. 14.
12. George M. Varnell, "Encore Puts Huskies in Select Company," *The Seattle Daily Times*, January 3, 1961, p. 17.
13. John J. Reddin, "Golden-Wedding Bells Ring For 'Coach' and 'Mother,'" *The Seattle Daily Times*, July 9, 1961, p. 19.
14. Ibid
15. Bob Johnson, "Varnell Returns 'Home,'" *The Spokane Daily Chronicle*, March 8, 1966, p. 11.
16. Ibid.
17. John J. Reddin, "Varnell Says Good-Bye," The Seattle Daily Times, August 21, 1966, p. 72.

BIBLIOGRAPHY

Ashe, Samuel A., Weeks, Stephen B., and Van Noppen, Charles L. (editors), *Biographical History of North Carolina: From Colonial Times to Present*, Greensboro, North Carolina: Charles L. Van Noppen, 1905.

Bamonte, Tony and Bamonte, Suzanne Schaeffer. *Spokane: Our Early History—Under All Is The Land*. Spokane, Washington: Tornado Creek, 2012

Bamonte, Tony and Bamonte, Suzanne Schaeffer. *Spokane's Legendary Davenport Hotel*. Spokane, Washington: Tornado Creek, 2001.

Borland, Lynn. *Pursuit of Perfection: Gilmore Dobie: From Orphanage to National Champion*. Tribute Publishing, 2010.

Brown, Daniel James. *The Boys in the Boat: Nine Americans and Their Epic Quest for Gold at the 1936 Berlin Olympics*. New York: Penguin Books, 2013.

Brown, Timothy P. *How Football Became Football: 150 Years of the Game's Evolution*. West Bloomfield, Michigan: Brown House Publishing, 2020.

Brownell, Sarah (editor). *The 1904 Anthropology Days and Olympic Games: Sport, Race, and American Imperialism*. Lincoln, Nebraska: University of Nebraska Press, 2008.

Coubertin, Pierre de. *Olympic Memoirs*. The International Olympic Committee, 1997.

Dunn, Edward B. *1121 Union: One Family's Story of Early Seattle's First Hill*. Seattle: Edward B. Dunn Historic Garden Trust, 2004.

Hughes, John. C. *Pressing On: Two Family-Owned Newspapers in the 21st Century*, Olympia, Washington: Office of the Secretary of State, 2015.

Kindersley, Dorling. *Chronicle of the Olympics: 1896-1996*. New York: DK Publishing, 1996.

Kumar, Amresh. *Complete Book of Olympic Games*. New Delhi: Khel Sahitya Kendra, 2007.

Lester, Robin. *Stagg's University*. Champaign, Illinois: University of Illinois Press, 1999.

Lindberg, Richard C. *The Gambler King of Clark Street*. Carbondale, Illinois: Southern Illinois University Press, 2009.

Mallon, Bill. *The 1904 Olympic Games: Results for All Competitors in All Events, with Commentary.* Jefferson, North Carolina: McFarland & Company, 1999.

Matthews, George and Marshall, Sandra. *St. Louis Olympics 1904.* Charleston, South Carolina: Arcadia Publishing, 2003.

Matthews, George R. *America's First Olympics: The St. Louis Games of 1904.* Columbia, Missouri: University of Missouri Press, 2005.

Nelson, David M. *The Anatomy of a Game: Football, the Rules, and the Men who Made the Game.* Cranbury, New Jersey: Associated University Presses, 1994.

Riess, Steven A. and Gems, Gerald R. *Chicago Sports Reader: 100 Years of Sports in the Windy City.* Champagne, Illinois: University of Illinois Press, 2009.

Robinson, Victor, ed. *Medical Review of Reviews.* New York: Boston Medical Library, 1918.

Schmidt, Raymond. *Shaping College Football: The Transformation of an American Sport, 1919-1930.* Syracuse, New York: Syracuse University Press, 2007.

Schoenberg, Wilfred P. *Gonzaga University: Seventy-five Years.* Gonzaga University, 1963.

Stanley, Gregory Kent. *Before Big Blue: Sports at the University of Kentucky 1880-1940.* Lexington, Kentucky: The University Press of Kentucky, 1996.

Stewart, Estelle May and Bowen, Jesse Chester. *History of Wages in the United States from Colonial Times to 1928.* Washington, D.C.: U.S. Printing Service, 1929.

Withers, Bud. *Glory Hounds: How a Small Northwest School Reshaped College Basketball and Itself.* Self-published, 2016.

Yeomans, Linda. *Patrick Henry & Virginia Beeson Miller Winston Houses.* 2013

INDEX

Dates
1882, 21, 170
1898, 22, 170
1899, 24, 33, 94, 170
1902, 4, 26, 33, 51, 77, 170
1904, 2–5, 26-28, 33-34, 36-37, 39-40, 42-45,47, 49, 51, 53-55, 57-59, 78-79, 81, 112-113, 170
1905, 2, 49, 59-61, 63, 66, 68, 89, 99, 170
1906, 5, 49, 69, 71-72, 90, 170
1907, 73, 79-80, 85, 91, 94-95, 102, 109, 166, 170
1908, xvi, 61, 90, 92--93, 96, 98-102, 106, 166, 170
1910, 70, 77, 107, 109-110, 119, 131, 139, 170
1911, 108, 111, 113, 170
1916, 93, 113-114, 119, 144, 171
1919, 120, 171
1922, 120-121, 123, 125, 132, 166, 171
1923, 121, 132, 139, 171
1925, 122, 124, 129-130, 132, 134-136, 139, 171
1927, 138, 140, 171
1936, ii, xvii, 133, 144, 149-151, 171
1937, 123, 145, 151, 171
1938, 157, 171
1946, 32, 123, 151, 171
1960, 158, 171
1966, 159-161, 171
1967, 164, 171

A
Aberdeen (Washington) High School, 84, 110, 119
Albemarle Times, The, 111
Albi, Joe, 90, 117, 167
Aleck, Charles (Basil Alexiev), 116
Almira High School, 101
Amateur Athletic Union, 4, 28
Anderson, Heartley "Hunk," 143-144
Anhalt, Frederick, 137
Archie, George, 152
Arthur, Chester, 112

B
Bagshaw, Enoch, 122
Baird, Charles, 50,

Baker, George, 93
Baker, Irene Stoddard, 26
Barnum, P.T., 140
Baxter, Portus, 139
Baylor, Elgin, 155
Bellingham Normal School, 92, 101
Bender, Johnny, 83-84, 87, 101
Berra, Lawrence Peter, 92
Bezdek, Hugo, 57, 114, 122
Bierman, Bernie, 158
Bishop, Ralph, 151
Blair Business College, 85, 92-95, 97-98
Blair, Clyde, 37, 59-60
Blethen, Bill, 145
Blethen, Clarence Brettun "C.B.," 132, 134
Blethen, Frank Sr., 136, 138, 160-161
Boarman, Marcus, 98, 100
Bockman, M.W., 28
Bohler, Fred, 99
Borland, Lynn, xvi
Borleske, Vincent, 97
"Boys in the Boat," The, ii, xvii, 132-133, 138, 149, 171
Brett, Bobby, 167
Brinker, Dode, 84
Broadway High School (Seattle), 138
Brougham, Royal, ii, 139-141, 150, 153
Brown, Bob, 111
Brown, Daniel James, ii, xvii, 149-150
Brown, Jim, 110
Brown, Johnny Mack, 123
Brown, Timothy P., i
Browne, John J., 106
Bulletin, The (Bend, Oregon), 126
Bullivant, Cisco, 80
Busch, Adolphus, 4
Butler, Mike "Dad," 36-37, 44, 60, 81

C
Callahan, Dr. T.E., 83-84
Callow, Russell "Rusty," 132, 135-136, 138
Calvert, Jane, 145
Camp, Walter, 33, 123-125, 171
Campbell-Hagerman College, 69-71
Canadeo, Tony, 166
Castleman, Frank, 43-44

ACKNOWLEDGEMENTS

First, I want to thank George Varnell's family—Patrick and Susan Dunn, Ned Dunn, Patty Carr, Virginia Varnell Dunn, Katherine Varnell Dunn, Sara Kirschenman, Michael Dunn, Carson Dunn, Oliver Sanders, Eden Sanders, Kate Sanders, and Rachael Sanders—for their partnership and for entrusting me to tackle the story of their amazing grandfather and great-grandfather. Thanks, also, to the exceptional research of Lori Larson, the remote assistance of Cole Paxton, and the wonderful editing of my almost-lifelong mentor and journalism hero, John C. Hughes.

Others to whom I am gratefully indebted for their help with this book include: Chuck Alm, Amy Anderson, Judy Anderson, Randy Anderson, Rick Anderson, Rick Arthur, Tony Bamonte, Suzanne Bamonte, Paul Barrett, Bruce Beale, Lynn Borland, Daniel James Brown, Susan M. Brown, Timothy P. Brown, Lisa Patterson Burlingame, Larry Cebula, Chicago History Museum, John Christianson, Eric Cohen, Christine Colburn, Charles R. Cross, Davenport Hotel, Riva Dean, Rodrigo DeMedeiros, Russ Dille, Brian Dirks, Sandy Deneau Dunham, Jasmin Edwards, Sandy Erickson, Kirsten Erwin, David Eskenazi, Cynthia Flash, Kelli Gieser, Gonzaga University, Dale Goodwin, Margo Greenman, Tren Griffin, Dan Grimm, Erica Hallock, Guy Harper, Dana Haynes, HistoryLink.org, Michael Houser, HuskyCrew.com, Richard Junger, David Kingma, Nicole Klein, Mel Kobel, Bob Kirlin, The Lacey PostNet, Steve Lundin, Adam Lyon, John Magnuson, Jean Gavin McCarthy, Melissa McCarthy, Larin McLaughlin, Mark Meadows, Daniel Meyer, Missouri Historical Society, Moonphoto, Shelby Rowe Moyer, Anuja Navare, Pasadena Museum of History, Lenville O'Donnell, Trova O'Heffernan, Joe Palmquist, Tierney Patterson, Julia Paulsen, Sally Paxton, Stephanie Plowman, Jim Price, Sammie Ragan, Paul Razore,

Lauren Sallwasser, Alex Schloer, Josh Schneider, *The Seattle Times*, Fay Smith, *The Spokane Daily Chronicle*, Spokane Public Library, *The Spokesman-Review*, Stanford University, Bill Steckel, Stewart Tilger, Peter Tormey, Transylvania University, Judy Rantz Willman, Ray Willman, University of Chicago, University of Washington, University of Washington Rowing, Ted Van Dyk, John L. Wilcox, Linda Yeomans, and Patricia Zcider.

Rodrigo DeMedeiros

ABOUT THE AUTHOR

Jeff Burlingame is the NAACP Image
Award-winning author of several
nonfiction books, and a recipient
of the Society of Professional
Journalists' prestigious Sigma Delta
Chi award. He and his family reside
in Tacoma, Washington.